AF306387

Decentralised digital security

Manchester University Press

INSCRIPTIONS

Series editors
Des Fitzgerald and Amy Hinterberger

Editorial advisory board
Vivette García Deister, National Autonomous University of Mexico
John Gardner, Monash University, Australia
Maja Horst, Technical University of Denmark
Robert Kirk, Manchester, UK
Stéphanie Loyd, Laval University, Canada
Alice Mah, Warwick University, UK
Deboleena Roy, Emory University, USA
Hallam Stevens, Nanyang Technological University, Singapore
Niki Vermeulen, Edinburgh, UK
Megan Warin, Adelaide University, Australia
Malte Ziewitz, Cornell University, USA

Since the very earliest studies of scientific communities, we have known that texts and worlds are bound together. One of the most important ways to stabilise, organise and grow a laboratory, a group of scholars, even an entire intellectual community, is to write things down. As for science, so for the social studies of science: Inscriptions is a space for writing, recording and inscribing the most exciting current work in sociological and anthropological – and any related – studies of science.

The series foregrounds theoretically innovative and empirically rich interdisciplinary work that is emerging in the UK and internationally. It is self-consciously hospitable in terms of its approach to discipline (all areas of social sciences are considered), topic (we are interested in all scientific objects, including biomedical objects) and scale (books will include both fine grained case studies and broad accounts of scientific cultures).

For readers, the series signals a new generation of scholarship captured in monograph form – tracking and analysing how science moves through our societies, cultures and lives. Employing innovative methodologies for investigating changing worlds, it is home to compelling new accounts of how science, technology, biomedicine and the environment translate and transform our social lives.

To buy or to find out more about the books currently available in this series, please go to: https://manchesteruniversitypress.co.uk/series/inscriptions-writing-the-social-studies-of-science/

Decentralised digital security

Code, crisis, community

Kelsie Nabben

MANCHESTER UNIVERSITY PRESS

Published by Manchester University Press
Oxford Road, Manchester, M13 9PL

www.manchesteruniversitypress.co.uk

British Library Cataloguing-in-Publication Data
A catalogue record for this book is available from the British Library

ISBN   978 1 5261 8709 3   hardback

First published 2026

The publisher has no responsibility for the persistence or accuracy of
URLs for any external or third-party internet websites referred to in this
book, and does not guarantee that any content on such websites is, or will
remain, accurate, accessible or appropriate.

EU authorised representative for GPSR:
Easy Access System Europe, Mustamäe tee 50, 10621 Tallinn, Estonia
gpsr.requests@easproject.com

Typeset
by Deanta Global Publishing Services, Chennai, India

Contents

Figures and tables

Figures

Tables

Acknowledgements

Thank you to Professor Ellie Rennie for encouraging me to write something new, as well as for the supervision, mentorship and feedback. Thank you to the team at the former RMIT University Blockchain Innovation Hub for supporting my academic journey. Thank you, Jeanne, for making this field study possible, and to each contributor to the Security Alliance, especially samczsun, Melanie from Discernible and security researcher Craig ('x86NOP'), for their feedback. Thank you also to Professor Jeffrey R. Yost, from the Charles Babbage Institute, and Dr Ben Carver, from the European University Institute, for feedback. Thank to the European University Institute Max Weber Fellowship programme, BlockchainGov/CNRS, and RMIT University for hosting me throughout my application for the book contract and manuscript writing. Research for this paper was funded by the Australian Research Council-funded Centre of Excellence for Automated Decision-Making and Society ('The Use of Automated Knowledge in Society' project). Thank you to the Ethereum Foundation for an ETH Rangers grant supporting my security research, which enabled me to recruit editing support and publish the book in Open Access. An incredible thank you to Cassidy Livingstone for edits. Thank you to Leah and Kerri for their family support so I could write; to my husband for accompanying me around the world with a baby so I could conduct data collection; to little E for expanding my capacity beyond measure; and to my father, Robert, who would be proud.

Introduction: the paradox of decentralised security

In the digital age, security is often imagined as a fixed state – something that can be achieved through the right combination of technology, policy and enforcement. The assumption has been that well-funded, centralised entities – whether tech companies, governments or cybersecurity firms – could safeguard digital environments through proactive risk mitigation and regulatory oversight. This model has critical limitations. Large-scale data breaches, corporate surveillance and vulnerabilities in cloud-based infrastructures have demonstrated that centralisation of digital infrastructure introduces systemic risks.

Decentralised technology security communities approach security not as a fixed end goal but as an ongoing process of adaptation, negotiation and contestation. Security in these contexts is as much social as it is technical, shaped by ideological commitments to cryptographic autonomy, the practical realities of infrastructural vulnerabilities and the constantly evolving landscape of cyber threats. This book examines how decentralised security is organised within blockchain ecosystems, tracing the structures, actors and motivations that underpin security practices in environments where traditional mechanisms of enforcement and accountability are limited. It explores how users, project teams and protocols collaborate – often across borders and jurisdictions – to confront both localised incidents and global security challenges.

Decentralised technologies were designed to eliminate the need for trust in intermediaries, offering a model of security rooted in the guarantees of cryptographic algorithms and software code rather than institutional oversight and enforcement. Paradoxically, decentralised systems remain insecure by default. From smart contract exploits to phishing attacks, to social engineering, to physical abductions and ransoms, security vulnerabilities and exploits – as detailed throughout this book – are a defining feature of Web3. Rather than achieving ideological visions of algorithmic governance, blockchain ecosystems reveal the extent to which *insecurity* is a persistent reality, made legible and addressable via collective processes that rely on a complex interplay of technical, economic, social and legal factors.

Through a digital ethnographic lens, this book interrogates the following question: what can decentralised technology communities teach us about digital security? It argues that decentralised security is best understood as the practice of making insecurity legible. Through various socio-technical infrastructures (including pre-agreed white hat rescue permissions, red-teaming drills, playbooks and incident command), decentralised communities govern what cannot be eliminated, offering insights for digital security in general.

At its core, this book argues that security in decentralised systems is not achieved merely through hardening code and other technical guarantees of security, but through collective efforts to coordinate and create infrastructure to navigate and address insecurity. This requires participants to cultivate a mindset of continual vigilance, a culture of coordination and sustainable incentives for the provision of security.

Weaving together anecdotal insights, participatory ethnographic observations and critical reflections, this book offers a grounded understanding of how decentralised security is organised, practised, experienced and contested. At a time when Web2 platforms face growing crises of data security, privacy and public trust, the practices emerging from decentralised Web3 communities offer valuable lessons more broadly for making digital insecurity legible.

As online life continues to expand, so too must our understanding of security not as an externally provisioned assurance but as a negotiated process of coordinating to address insecurity that spans individual responsibility, code, commerce and community. These insights point to governance of security by visibility – a social and technical pursuit of instruments, norms and lessons, sustained through collective responsibility.

Security and decentralised technologies

When I place my email address in the website 'Have I Been Pwned' (meaning 'have I been hacked?'), the answer for me, like for many others, is yes. I've had that email address for years. It's been implicated in numerous data hacks, including a recruitment database for the Australian government, a major health insurance provider, a major airline and the Internet Archive not-for-profit digital library. Breaches like this demonstrate that whilst the future is digital, it's unclear how well this works for people.

Evidently, the digital infrastructure I engage with on a day-to-day basis is not secure. In the same way, modern digital infrastructure provides insufficient security guarantees for banks, social platform providers and governments. Digital interactions in these contexts rely on institutions as the centralised guarantors of security, which are often unable to offer recourse (to be fair, the airline gave me some 'status credits'). Financial scams and data hacks are losses that both the institution and the user bear the cost of. It is from these discontents that the ideology of open-source, decentralised technologies emerged.

The central focus of this book is security, specifically the security of digital infrastructure. Without security, digital economies are not possible. This assertion anchors the central argument of this book: that insecurity characterises each interaction and transaction in digital space, and addressing insecurity is a foundational condition for the formation, maintenance and legitimacy of digital economies. As explored throughout this book, the responsibility and consequences of security are often unevenly distributed, raising critical questions about who defines security, who is protected and at what cost. In this context, understanding how security is implemented, sustained, experienced and politicised is essential to making sense of digital economies as socio-technical systems.

To examine the topic of digital security in depth, I focus on decentralised technologies. Security, in this context, is a multifaceted concept that encompasses technical, social, infrastructural, legal and economic dimensions. What is being secured includes data, communications, exchange, value and ultimately, people. Technical security pertains to the integrity, confidentiality and reliability of digital systems through cryptographic mechanisms like public key cryptography[1] and consensus algorithms,[2] as well as protection against technical vulnerabilities, such as hacks, exploits and bugs in software code. Social security refers to the collective, human efforts to secure decentralised systems, including organisation, governance and coordination among geographically dispersed communities. This involves individuals, groups and institutions working to anticipate and address vulnerabilities, including those arising from social engineering (the manipulation of people – rather than systems or software – to gain unauthorised access to data, systems or assets). Infrastructural security concerns the robustness and reliability of the hardware and software foundations that support decentralised systems. This includes how vulnerabilities in hardware production, supply chains or consensus participants expose decentralised systems to risks – from servers to geopolitical dependencies. In terms of economics, security provision is driven by incentives. All of these facets must occur within legal bounds, and be subject to legal repercussions.

Security is fundamental to digital economies. By foregrounding blockchain security as both infrastructure and practice, this book contends that digital economies depend not just on cryptography or code, but on the social and technical practices that make insecurity legible and addressable. By documenting the landscape, stakeholders and practices involved, this book shows how decentralised technology communities help us to rethink digital security – not as the elimination of vulnerability, but as a practice expressed through infrastructure that makes insecurity legible; norms that define who gets to act and on what terms; controls that implement and govern decisions; and reviews that surface lessons and improve awareness and tools. Its reflections articulate how such negotiations reshape our understanding of what digital security is, how it is organised and who is responsible for its practice and maintenance.

What are 'decentralised' technologies?

Decentralised technologies, including public blockchain systems, are a subset of a distributed system those with a physically distributed network architecture where multiple authorities control different components, and no authority is fully trusted by all (Troncoso *et al.*, 2017). Decentralisation includes the full technology stack of hardware, open-source software code,[3] cryptography and decentralised applications, with the aim of providing participants with opportunities to own, operate, govern and maintain all components of an infrastructure according to a specified rule set (Nabben and Zargham, 2022).

The decentralisation of technologies refers to a social and technical phenomenon, whereby the social, political, economic and legal dynamics of a system are decentralised, as well as its technical architecture (Buterin, 2017; Calvão, 2018; Bodó and Giannopoulou, 2020; Bodó *et al.*, 2021). In a decentralised paradigm, the design and operation of a technology are geographically and computationally distributed among participants in a network, meaning that participants collectively operate and maintain the infrastructure, and (often theoretically), no single actor controls it. Although there are many distributed technologies that precede public blockchains (such as BitTorrent and other peer-to-peer networks), this book examines blockchain technology as a prime example of what is meant by 'decentralised technologies'. The origins of Bitcoin as the first fully functioning, decentralised peer-to-peer blockchain protocol can, in part, be attributed to a countercultural group known as the Cypherpunks (as discussed in Chapter 2). In contrast to the traditional internet and Web2 applications,[4] decentralised networks provide an alternative paradigm for people to coordinate. This book explores the affordances[5] of decentralised digital technologies in relation to security, as well as the challenges of securing distributed digital infrastructures.

Public, permissionless blockchains operate as a form of private governance, similar to other extra-legal domains (such as gangs, pirates and prisons) (Jaspers, 2017), relying on self-regulation and private enforcement to maintain order (Stringham, 2017: 320). While blockchain networks function as club goods, the security they provide resembles a public good – non-rivalrous and non-excludable – yet it is provisioned through private actors like security firms, auditors and white hat hackers. Unlike traditional private governance, however, blockchain as an industry and an ideology aims to decentralise the provision of security by supporting coordination and open resources among a distributed network of participants.

Without central authorities to enforce trust, decentralised systems rely on cryptographic protocols, consensus mechanisms and incentive structures to ensure that data remains tamper-proof, transactions are valid and participants behave honestly in line with the rules of the system. Perceptions of security vulnerabilities in decentralised technologies vary widely depending on the underlying consensus model of a blockchain software protocol. Proof of Work, used by Bitcoin, is often seen as highly secure due to its computational cost and resistance to Sybil attacks, though concerns about mining centralisation persist. In contrast, Proof of Stake models, like Ethereum's post-Merge design, are more energy-efficient but raise concerns about wealth concentration, validator collusion and new forms of governance risk. Emerging models such as Solana's Proof of History, which prioritise speed and throughput, introduce other vulnerabilities – particularly around validator centralisation and fault tolerance. Ultimately, different levels of decentralisation in the consensus mechanism of a protocol create distinct trade-offs between resilience, efficiency and trust, with security emerging not solely from code, but from the broader social, economic and infrastructural arrangements in which consensus is embedded. Furthermore, blockchain-based decentralised organisations (i.e. Decentralised Autonomous Organisations, or DAOs, which leverage blockchain functionality for collective decision-making), introduce new classes of vulnerabilities. These include governance attacks that exploit flaws in voting mechanisms, incentive and/or identity and reputation structures (Nabben, 2024).

The sheer number of blockchain projects also characterises the security landscape, with over one hundred projects with significant market capitalisation and user bases, and more than ten thousand in total. On one hand, this proliferation fosters innovation and experimentation with different applications, governance models and incentive structures. On the other hand, it fragments attention, talent and security resources. Many projects lack the funding, technical expertise or size to maintain robust security practices, making them vulnerable to exploitation. Attackers often target smaller or newer chains or applications where defences are weaker. The result is a diverse but uneven security landscape, where security externalities are increasingly common, for example, vulnerabilities in one protocol cascading into others through 'bridges' between blockchains or shared software code libraries or tooling. This scale and diversity demand significant resources, not only to ensure technical safeguards, but also to facilitate coordination via threat intelligence sharing and incident post-mortem insights across the broader blockchain ecosystem.

Web2 v. Web3

Today's mainstream paradigm for digital life is known as Web2, and is characterised by centralised, 'Big Tech' companies and their inherent flaws – from data insecurity to commodification of users (Birch *et al.*, 2021). This framework of digital interaction is defined by a platform-based internet where centralised entities (like Google, Facebook and Amazon) control data, infrastructure and user interactions. It is driven by user-generated content, social networking and cloud-based services, but also by platform monopolies and data extraction.

In the Web2 era, security is largely centralised, managed by institutions that wielded control over data, access and enforcement. The assumption was that well-funded, centralised entities – whether tech companies, governments or cybersecurity firms – could safeguard digital environments through proactive risk mitigation and regulatory oversight. However, this model has revealed critical limitations. Large-scale data breaches, corporate surveillance and vulnerabilities in cloud-based infrastructures have demonstrated that centralisation itself introduces systemic risks.

In contrast, Web3 represents a shift towards decentralised infrastructure and governance through cryptographic technologies such as public blockchains (Nabben, 2023a). The ideological, technical and security dynamics of Web3 decentralised technologies stem from the cryptographic core of the technology that can provide computational guarantees to secure digital interactions, in areas from communication to commerce. However, Web3 transcends mere technological innovation to encompass socio-political and governance transformations where communities experiment with new forms of organisation, economic coordination and security. Web3 promotes a vision of more 'user-sovereign' digital networks, where individuals control their identities, assets and decision-making through decentralised protocols and the participatory governance arrangements they afford.

An economic lens aids in understanding the evolving security landscape of the internet and its decentralised successors. In Web1 and Web2, network security suffered from classic negative externalities. The costs of insecure systems such as spam, malware and Distributed Denial of Service (DDoS) attacks (see Chapter 2) were rarely borne by those responsible, creating a misalignment between individual incentives and collective security. Anderson argues that security is ultimately about incentives (often perverse incentives, such as network externalities, asymmetric information, moral hazard, liability dumping and tragedy of the commons), and resource scarcity helps to explain why underinvestment in security is so persistent (Anderson, 2001). Blockchain and Web3 architectures attempt to re-engineer these dynamics by embedding economic incentives directly into protocols. Through mechanisms like slashing, staking and composable rewards, they aim to internalise the externalities and make secure behaviour economically rational. Yet, while Web3 aspires to return control of data and assets to users, decentralised, public blockchain ledgers introduce fresh avenues for exploitation.

The key question of security

Cybersecurity is at the frontier of digital network governance (DeNardis, 2014). At the heart of this book lies the question: what can decentralised technology communities teach us about digital security? This question drives an exploration of the practices, relationships and paradoxes that characterise security in decentralised systems. The aim of this question, and thus this book, is to uncover how decentralised communities create and secure their digital infrastructure, and in turn, what decentralised security can teach us about improving digital security more broadly.

Decentralised technologies require a different security paradigm to traditional, Web2 cybersecurity. There are important distinctions about the nature of network security in decentralised architectures compared to traditional network security. Decentralisation can enhance resilience against certain types of attacks (i.e. single points of failure); however, it also introduces complexities such as questions about the level of responsibility of system designers as opposed to users for security, the existence of irreversible transactions with no consumer guarantees and the system risks of cascade effects across protocols in the case of failure (such as a tanked cryptocurrency token price).

Analysing the efforts and challenges of building, governing and maintaining secure digital infrastructure in a decentralised context reveals the insecurity of digital networks. While traditional cybersecurity often follows the principle of creating a secure perimeter and managing access, blockchain security focuses on ensuring the integrity and 'trustlessness' of transactions and interactions in the absence of a central authority to enforce good behaviour.[6] Furthermore, both contexts are subject to an evolving regulatory landscape; however traditional networks often have clearer regulatory and compliance frameworks, while blockchain regulators are still navigating guidance, making compliance a more complex matter in decentralised contexts. Yet, the coproduction of infrastructures and norms to make insecurity visible, coordinate action and disseminate insights provides reproducible lessons about digital security beyond Web3.

Digital ethnographic methodology

This book utilises digital ethnography to examine how security is enacted in decentralised systems. While ethnography studies people, practice and meaning in situ, digital ethnography recognises that these relations are organised through online infrastructures (Hine, 2000; Pink *et al.*, 2016). Ethnography reveals the lived experiences and practices that underpin digital security (Shires, 2018; Monsees, 2020; Tanczer, 2020). My approach combined sustained observation of digital channels with research interviews and participation in security practice drills, incident discussions and governance. A brief intellectual history (see Gilbert, 1971; Whatmore, 2016) that draws on primary and secondary sources (for example, the Cypherpunk Mailing List archives, [Cryptoanarchy.wiki, 1992–98]) is included in Chapter 2 to situate current practices by tracing how ideas about cryptography and decentralisation inform cryptocurrency cultures today.

Becoming 'crypto-native'[7] was necessary for in-depth and credible participant observation. I used on-(block)chain tools, engaged in Discord, Telegram and X (formerly Twitter) discussions, followed DAO processes and attended peak crypto-security industry events 'IRL' (in real life). Becoming crypto-native thus enabled a form of participant observation attuned to the decentralised and pseudonymous nature (of others, not me as a declared researcher) of blockchain life. This immersion made it possible to grasp how security is lived, contested and co-produced across technical, social and economic domains in Web3.

The primary field site was the Security Alliance (or SEAL, as a play on both the name and Navy SEALs as elite emergency responders) (Security Alliance, n.d.a). SEAL is a not-for-profit organisation backed by private donors, blockchain foundations and venture capital firms coordinating across multiple blockchain ecosystems (with a centre of gravity in Ethereum).[8] Founded by the blockchain-famous white hat hacker samczsun and expert collaborators (including blockchain projects, security firms, independent security contributors, blockchain foundations, venture capitalists and more), SEAL launched publicly in February 2024 with a number of flagship initiatives (detailed in Chapter 4) that seek to improve social coordination among a distributed security ecosystem (see Chapter 3) and address key issues on technical infrastructure for security, legal guarantees for good faith hackers and emergency response for blockchain users. My access to white hat and security professional communication channels afforded exceptional visibility into concerns, priorities, wins and frustrations. It also risked influencing me to over-identify with one moral frame. I mitigated this by triangulating claims (for example, hack event post-mortems, industry statistics and reports, government statements and individual interviews). I treat the label of white hat descriptively (what actors call themselves) and analytically (how that claim is accepted or refused), not normatively as a moral endorsement, with the goal to highlight the paradoxes and challenges that occur in provisioning decentralised security.

Data collection for this book occurred under university ethics approval between September 2023, in the lead-up to the launch of SEAL, and the aftermath of the April 2025 major cryptocurrency hack (detailed in Chapter 6). Data was collected via online chat channels and offline forums. Online materials included public and private group chats on the application Telegram, open-source software repositories on the platform GitHub, public posts on the social media platform X, as well as internal and external blockchain project documentation. Offline channels included semi-structured interviews via video call or Telegram, conference sessions, workshops and informal meetings. I also participated in several SEAL initiatives (including drill coordination and documentation for SEAL Wargames, technical writing for SEAL-ISAC, and providing feedback and GitHub repo commits on SEAL Frameworks). A full draft was circulated to participants for quote verification in context, as per the ethics agreement. No analytical changes to the content of the manuscript or omissions were required in response to this.

This methodology bridges social and technical analysis by following how actors make insecurity legible and coordinate under pressure. It privileges situated practice over retrospective idealisation or baseless critique, acknowledging both the access advantages and interpretive limitations that accompany embedded research in a dynamic, highly paranoid pseudonymous domain.

Entering the field (a story of reluctance and re-engagement)

In some ways, my position as a researcher in relation to blockchain communities is a story of reluctance. I had been trying to 'quit' crypto for years. Having gone down the 'crypto rabbit hole' in my twenties, I met someone in an elevator at a conference who offered me a job to work on something big, and I took it. I swiftly found myself relocating to Bangkok, Thailand, for a year to work for one of the largest initial coin offering (ICO) projects in the world. At the time it raised $12 million, and now it no longer exists. Fast forward six years, and I had come full circle. I was back where it all began in Bangkok – no longer the naive girl who was easily convinced to uproot my life for work – but pursuing intellectual curiosities all the same. This time, for the 'DeFi' (Decentralised Finance) Security Summit (DSS) and the world's largest Ethereum blockchain developer conference – 'DevCon'. This experience six years ago had led me down a path of observation and experience, including travelling one week per month to cryptocurrency conferences around the world, Ubering minibuses with co-founder of Ethereum Vitalik Buterin and his Ethereum Foundation developer friends and seeing the rise of fall of various projects, including the one that I was employed by shortly after I resigned and moved back to Australia to be closer to family.

This time, I was returning to Bangkok for data collection for this book to attend the DeFi Security Summit (DSS) – the peak industry conference on blockchain security – to participate in SEAL events, gather research data and test research findings. I had a PhD on 'resilience' in decentralised technologies but still much to learn in this ever-evolving arena. Travelling to DSS was pivotal for my research endeavours on decentralised, digital security to meet and experience the industry in person following months of digitally mediated data collection.[9] Despite having my young family in tow, I was no longer reluctant, as these experiences were formative in my research and understanding of how decentralised technology communities are changing what digital security can mean, as well as a trip down memory lane into the wild world of blockchain.

Engaging with SEAL as an academic researcher was tense at first. The general sentiment was that if privacy or confidentiality was broken, or inappropriate interruptions or actions to this security subculture were displayed, access would be revoked. As part of the process to gain ethical consent to conduct research, an early SEAL contributor instructed me:

> Not many things can get you kicked out of SEAL/inner circle but breaking confidentiality is one of them...because trust is the most important thing we have. Trusting and respecting each other even if we don't always agree. So keep what is said/discussed private and if you leak know that I will find out.

While participation in blockchain protocols according to pre-prescribed rule sets is accessible to anyone (known as 'permissionless'), security groups are not. Instead, they are predominantly pseudonymous, meaning reputation is built on past behaviours as a predictor of future success. A core contributor's message in the SEAL chat stated: 'SEAL is not permissionless...Everyone here has power to shape our internet's future which is an honour, but also a responsibility'.

The first online chat group calls I joined were in relation to the planning and live exercise of a SEAL Wargames attack simulation.[10] The request was to 'just observe and don't say a word...because no-one is supposed to be there'. As is typical with cryptocurrency research, contributions of labour were in demand (Nabben and Zargham, 2022). Once they found out that academics have skills that could be useful for their cause (including writing, editing and general operational support), I was roped into an administrative role to support with basic tasks, such as scheduling Wargames exercises and drafting documentation. This granted access to the invitation-only group chat of SEAL, which enabled me to observe and participate in a number of other SEAL initiatives.

Theoretical foundations: security as a socio-technical phenomenon

Security is not solely technical but deeply socio-technical, meaning the social and technical are co-constitutive (they shape one another) and inextricably linked (Bijker and Law, 1994). Researchers have shown how cybersecurity governance can be made visible by foregrounding non-traditional actors, their actions and politics (Dunn Cavelty and Wenger, 2000; Nissenbaum, 2009; Stevens, 2020; Tanczer, 2020). Indeed, what is meant by 'cybersecurity' remains highly contested, and different groups reference the concept to advocate for different things, from privacy and encryption access rights to free markets and private actor responsibility for privacy measures, to stronger state regulation and control (Wolff, 2016; Liebetrau and Monsees, 2022). This book unpacks security in practice to show how security is collaboratively produced, maintained and contested within decentralised technology communities.

Blockchain and decentralised systems are designed to operate without centralised control, yet the functioning of these systems is inseparable from the communities that create, maintain and govern them. Developers, miners, validators, white hat hackers and users all play roles in shaping decentralised infrastructures, highlighting the interplay between code, hardware and human labour. This socio-technical perspective reveals how security in decentralised technologies is both a technical concern and a product of collective, often less visible social effort. Thus, this book is not concerned with 'solving' cybersecurity but with understanding the social dimensions of digital security for those that participate in digital networks.

Infrastructure as theoretical framing

The conceptual framing of 'infrastructuring' provides theoretical scaffolding that supports the narrative of the book. Infrastructure studies address the technical, social and organisational aspects of the development, usage and maintenance of infrastructure in local communities or at a global scale (Bowker *et al.*, 2009). Technology is defined as a material, method or tool. Infrastructures, on the other hand, are the structures that technologies create when they are composed by groups of people for specific purposes (Jewett and Kling, 1991; Star, 1999). 'Information' infrastructures are digital facilities and services, including human and computer protocols such as the internet, whose functional purpose is revealed by their use (Star and Ruhleder, 1996).

By extension, 'infrastructuring' describes the ongoing processes by which stakeholders design, build, maintain and adapt infrastructure (Star and Bowker, 2010; Collier, 2018; Liebetrau and Christensen, 2021). This framing extends to the study of security by attending to how communities come together to build, maintain and govern decentralised infrastructures.

Scholars argue that 'good' information infrastructure is one that is constructed with awareness of the social and political context the infrastructure is operating in, offers stable support for its intended function and is flexible and modifiable at both the technical and social levels (Star and Bowker, 2010). Navigating this in practice involves understanding how these technologies facilitate new community formations, economic models and social movements that diverge from traditional institutional models to serve the interests of stakeholders.

This framing draws on the literature on blockchain as an institutional infrastructure and object of social inquiry (Berg *et al.*, 2019; Hayes, 2019; Kow and Lustig, 2018). Bitcoin, for example, offers a model of collective infrastructural governance, a mode of cooperative interdependence between infrastructures and their users, maintainers, or other systems, where both sides benefit and sustain each other over time (Swartz, 2018). Its governance occurs both via the infrastructure of the Bitcoin protocol itself, as well as of the infrastructure by the community of developers and other stakeholders (De Filippi and Loveluck, 2016). Building upon these ideas, this book illuminates infrastructuring practices of security occurring within decentralised technological communities to provide generalisable insights about how insecurity can be made legible.

Speculation, critique and paradox

Much of the existing discourse on decentralised technology communities is predicated on binary approaches of speculation or critique. Speculative takes tend to celebrate key figures in the blockchain industry, portraying them as visionaries who champion digital freedom, emphasising the ever-rising token prices and extraordinary financial success, as well as the promises of technological innovation (Hoyng, 2023). Critical perspectives argue that the cryptocurrency industry perpetuates and reinforces existing economic and technocratic inequalities and lack of progress regarding user experience (Marlinspike, 2022; O'Dwyer, 2015). Some critiques also highlight the environmental costs of the high computational power required to maintain distributed networks (Wendl *et al.*, 2023).[11]

This book moves beyond polarised or premeditated judgements to engage with blockchain communities through an ethnographic mode of inquiry, examining how security, coordination and governance emerge or fall short in practice. Rather than focusing on ideological debates or deterministic narratives, the following pages will foreground the lived experiences of developers, users, white hat hackers and other blockchain security stakeholders as they navigate the complexities of decentralised infrastructures. By doing so, it offers a grounded analysis of the socio-technical conditions that shape blockchain security, uncovering how technical protocols, ideological impetus, governance mechanisms and economic incentives interact within distributed systems in relation to security.

That being said, decentralised security is encompassed by the common thread of paradox. Scholars highlight that to understand infrastructure means acknowledging its paradoxical nature (Howe *et al.*, 2016). For example, infrastructure is generative but degenerates, solid but temporal and created to mitigate risk while introducing new risks (Howe *et al.*, 2016). Identifying and acknowledging the paradoxes of decentralised infrastructures reveals more about their attributes, affordances and cultures. For example, in a post on X, co-founder of the prominent Ethereum public blockchain, Vitalik Buterin, signals that his belief in the viability of decentralised technologies creates an array of paradoxes: 'some still open contradictions in my thoughts and my values, that I have been thinking about but still don't feel like I've fully resolved' (vitalik.eth, 2022). A central paradox of decentralised technologies: while they offer an infrastructure built on cryptographic privacy and security, they remain fundamentally insecure due to the inherent vulnerabilities of digital infrastructure and the behaviours of users that enable hacks, scams and fraud. As this book demonstrates, blockchain is dependent on the security industry, white hat fund rescuers and even the involvement of traditional police and law enforcement agencies to address insecurity.

Moral economies and boundary work in white hat security

This book also introduces and documents the activities of 'white hat hackers' as protagonists in the blockchain security landscape. White hat hacking is not a fixed role but a situated identity produced through boundary work. Boundary work names the practical labour of drawing, defending and revising the lines that separate legitimate from illegitimate actors and actions, determining how communities claim authority, resources and the right to intervene (Gieryn, 1983). As demonstrated in adjacent hacker communities, technical craft travels with moral imaginaries: claims to do good are enacted, disputed and policed in practice (Coleman and Golub, 2008). In decentralised security, boundary work is visible in 'good-faith' tests (such as responsible disclosures, post-mortem incident reporting and reward fee transparency), access decisions (such as who is admitted to war rooms, security advisory councils or multisignature wallet signers) and sanctions (i.e. public callouts for misbehaviour or exclusion from certain channels or forums).

Adjacently, boundary objects are the artefacts that carry this work across otherwise disjoint 'social worlds' (Star and Griesemer, 1989). In the context of security, boundary objects include security frameworks, help tickets, intelligence dashboards, blocklists, incident-command checklists, on-chain attestations and post-mortem reports. They are flexible enough for local interpretation yet standardised enough to travel across projects, firms and jurisdictions – including among pseudonymous participants – thereby coordinating action without requiring consensus on values or identity. Taken together, boundary work and boundary objects are the glue of decentralised security's legibility regime: they render insecurity visible, sortable and actionable, while also revealing the politics of who gets to see, decide and intervene.

In this book, the term 'white hat' names a moving target – assembled through successful rescues, disclosure etiquette, channel gatekeeping and post-mortem narration and communication. These practices stabilise the category of white hat, making it usable under the tension of live fund rescues while remaining contestable when conduct drifts or rogue actors attempt to infiltrate its scripts. The point is not to certify white hats as virtuous or sinister but to analyse how, amid persistent insecurity, communities make interventions legible, and then justify, motivate and govern who gets to act and in what ways. This moral and organisational work, with all of its successes, frictions and shortcomings, teaches us about how digital security is enacted and governed in the wild.

Technology, infrastructure and the future of law

In 1997, computer scientist and Cypherpunk Mark Miller articulated a vision of 'computer security as the future of law' that remains relevant to the plight of decentralised technologies as secure, digital infrastructure for human interaction. The idea extends Lawrence Lessig's argument that 'code is law': that in digital environments, software code functions as a form of regulation in a similar way that legal rules do in the physical world in terms of structuring, constraining and enabling behaviour through architectural controls that are embedded in software itself (Lessig, 1999: 1). Thus, those who write and control code (i.e. developers, platform owners and protocol designers) wield regulatory power to determine what users can and cannot do, who has access and under what conditions. Blockchain communities have, to some extent, (mis)appropriated the phrase 'code is law' to suggest that algorithmic governance is superior to other forms of bureaucratic authority (Hassan and De Filippi, 2017). Lessig rightfully points out that whilst code is the architecture of the internet, online spaces are governed by a combination of law (formal rules backed by the state), market (economic incentives and pressures) and norms (social expectations and informal rules) (Lessig, 1999).

Miller's idea of computer security as the future of law extends the idea of code as law – contending that those who write code control security. Miller argued that computer security mechanisms would increasingly assume functions traditionally managed by legal systems, particularly in governing digital interactions (Miller, 2017). As such, Miller envisions a future where computational security architectures replace or complement legal frameworks by automating compliance and dispute resolution while embedding enforceable rules directly into digital systems. This vision is embodied in public blockchain protocols.

In decentralised systems especially, where state law may not be enforceable, security infrastructure effectively becomes the default mode of governance and recourse (or lack thereof). Miller suggests that by designing computational systems for 'secure cooperation' via enforcing permissions and constraints at the code level, digital infrastructure can provide security, accountability and economic coordination without reliance on centralised authorities (2017). Yet, to enact this vision requires underlying software architecture to be secure.

Conclusion

By investigating the security practices occurring in decentralised technology communities, the ethnographies presented throughout this book illuminate how digitisation itself is a form of insecurity. The emergence of decentralised digital infrastructure is concerned not only with enacting certain ideologies of non-state money but with designing and maintaining secure digital ecosystems that surpass the social, political and technical limitations of Web2. Thus, insecurity is addressed not just from technical systems or economic incentives but from the interplay between technical systems, economic incentives and social practices. This book makes the argument that by making insecurity legible, and thus addressable, decentralised communities govern what cannot be eliminated.

The analysis unfolds in four parts. Part I, 'The foundations of decentralised security', traces the ideological and technical underpinnings of blockchain security, highlighting how cryptography, privacy and autonomy are essential to decentralised digital economies. Part II, 'How decentralised security is organised', examines the actors, infrastructures and incentives that shape security practices in Web3 – from the structural insecurity of digital infrastructure to the emergent role of white hat hackers and collaborative security initiatives they coordinate. Part III, 'Decentralised digital security at scale', expands the analysis to the material and geopolitical foundations of blockchain security with a focus on physical and the Democratic Republic of North Korea, considering how external threats, regulatory pressures, jurisdictional limitations and industry self-regulation interact. Finally, Part IV, 'Securing digital futures', synthesises the 'Critical lessons for the future of decentralised security', outlining the core imperatives of addressing insecurity across decentralised ecosystems while maintaining the ethos of openness and autonomy, as well as the many challenges remaining.

The following chapter examines the ideological foundations and historical origins of decentralised technologies, which are critical for understanding the security practices that have emerged within these communities. By situating contemporary practices within their broader socio-technical and ideological contexts, the book establishes a foundation for analysing how decentralised communities organise, negotiate and sustain security in the face of persistent insecurity.

Notes

1 Public key cryptography, also known as asymmetric encryption, is a method of securing digital communications and transactions using a public key (public passcode) and a private key (secret passcode) that

allows for secure communication between parties without needing to share a secret key in advance. It is widely used in applications like secure email, online banking and cryptocurrencies (e.g. Bitcoin and Ethereum) to protect transactions and verify identities.

2 Consensus algorithms, as methods used to ensure that all participants (or nodes) agree on a shared state or record of transactions, determine the governance of distributed systems. In the absence of a central authority, these algorithms help maintain the security and integrity of a system by ensuring that only valid transactions are recorded. Common types of consensus algorithms in blockchain networks include Proof of Work (as used in Bitcoin, where miners expend computational power to solve complex mathematical puzzles to validate transactions and add blocks to the chain) and Proof of Stake, where validators 'stake' cryptocurrency as collateral to participate in validating transactions, as in Ethereum 2.0.

3 Open-source software means that anyone has the right to access, make and distribute copies and improve the software. See Perens, 1999.

4 Web2 refers to the second generation of the internet. It marked a shift from static, read-only web pages (Web 1.0) to interactive, user-generated, and social platforms. It emerged in the early 2000s and laid the foundation for the digital ecosystems we use today.

5 The lens of 'affordances' refers to how artefacts, including technologies, 'request, demand, allow, encourage, discourage, and refuse' (Davis and Chouinard, 2016: 241). This framing allows me to ask not *what* affordances decentralised technologies as artefacts have, but what the mechanisms are of *how* these artefacts afford, and *for whom* and *under what circumstances* (or conditions) these artefacts afford (Davis and Chouinard, 2016). See: Davis, 2020; Davis and Chouinard, 2016.

6 Trustlessness in blockchain-based systems refers to the confidence to transact with a stranger based on the guarantees of a decentralised technical infrastructure, rather than enforcement of rules by a centralised authority. Thus, 'trustless' means that you don't need to trust any individual participant – you can trust the system as a whole, because it is designed to be transparent, tamper-resistant and governed by code. See also: De Filippi *et al.*, 2020.

7 The term 'crypto-native' emerged within the Ethereum blockchain community around the late 2010s, gaining traction around what is known as the 'DeFi (Decentralised Finance) summer' of 2020, when people began living 'on-chain', meaning learning, investing, building and governing through crypto applications, as opposed to relying on

traditional finance (TradFi). The phrase has become a way to signal belonging within Web3 communities by marking a contrast with 'Web2 mindsets' or 'normie' behaviour, where users are seen as external to or unfamiliar with decentralised systems.

8 See later anecdotes and analysis on reliance on white hats to secure users' bags, as well as white hat motivations.

9 Note: some travel costs were supported by an Ethereum Foundation DevCon 2024 academic grant.

10 SEAL Wargames is a security drill practice service provided by SEAL. See: Nabben and De Filippi, 2023.

11 However, these concerns are often conflated, as environmental sustainability is crucial to the legitimacy of blockchains (Rennie, 2024). For example, some large-scale Bitcoin mining operations rely on clean energy sources. Other protocols such as Ethereum have successfully undertaken a landmark transition from Proof of Work, which relies on energy-intensive computation to secure the network, to Proof of Stake, where security is maintained through financial commitments rather than computational expenditure.

Part I

Foundations of decentralised security

1

The principles of decentralised security

Introduction

Security is a prerequisite for digital economies as it lays the foundational conditions for trust, exchanges of data and coordination. This chapter provides an intellectual history of digital security, setting out conceptual elements that are fundamental to understanding security in decentralised digital context. It is organised according to three historical eras.[1] The first era is defined by the computer hackers of the 1960s, who demonstrated hacking as a counterculture of individual freedom through making and breaking computers. The second era revolves around the public key cryptographers of the 1970s, as well as the Xanadu and American Information Exchange (AMiX) communities of the 1980s, who contributed to early ideas on the development of economic commerce, highlighting the need for secure means of digital exchange. The third era highlights the Cypherpunks of the 1990s, a disparate group of privacy advocates who authored the 'Cypherpunk Manifesto' and used computer code and cryptography to build secure, decentralised digital infrastructures. Their aim was to wield the power of cryptography and computers to resist state and corporate surveillance and enable individual autonomy.

Each of these historical phases highlights the technical, social, economic and cultural conditions that gave rise to public blockchain technology as we know it. Throughout its historical developments, we see decentralisation and security as evolving social and political concepts.[2] Rather than providing a comprehensive history – which would require a book of its own – these accounts are intentionally partial and imperfect, reflecting the fragmented and improvisational nature of the maker-breaker-hacker cultures they depict. Thus, my intention in this chapter is to introduce key concepts and provide the fundamental framing for the remainder of this book on decentralised security.

By highlighting core historical developments in the field, this chapter positions security as a contested and politicised concept, revealing public blockchains as a socio-political phenomenon of ideological and governance claims, rather than a strictly technical domain. In this context, decentralisation reconfigures the concept of security into one of *insecurity*, based on a worldview that is predicated on distrust, surveillance and paranoia. Through this analysis, this chapter lays the groundwork for understanding the broader landscape of security challenges and solutions occurring in decentralised technology communities today.

A cryptographic exchange

I wasn't really sure how I got invited to a squatter house party in Prague on an evening of the Ethereum community's largest annual developer conference, 'DevCon'. Up until this point, sheer curiosity had led me 'down the rabbit hole' of the crypto (cryptocurrency) industry – as seemed to be the story of many others as well. This night took me a little further down that path…

The squatter house was run down. The crowd was a motley mix of developer-types in jeans and branded t-shirts, men dressed in all black, and a few goth-looking women involved in privacy protocols and outer space startups. I tried to stay close to at least one of the familiar faces I had entered with and avoid the toilet. Before I had made it into the depths of the house or out to the backyard, I got talking to a man in the corridor who was wearing his child's fairy wings over an unbranded orange t-shirt and jeans. Partway through the general conversation, he asked for my handle on the chat application Telegram (which is popular in cryptocurrency circles).

'@kelsienabben', I responded, without thinking much of it.[3] 'Is that your real name??', he scoffed. I didn't understand why that was so shocking. I was a nobody here. What did I have to hide? 'Mine is Martin Smith', he said. As I wandered away to explore what more the house had to offer, I wondered why I was the out of place one between us when he was wearing fairy wings, who he was if 'Mr Smith' wasn't his real name, and whether I should change my handle on Telegram.

Approximately two years later, I had another encounter with 'Martin'. This time, it was at the semi-regular 'WEB3 HACK' meetup in my local city on a Thursday night.[4] The special guest speaker via video link was 'Zooko'; well-known cryptographer, self-proclaimed Cypherpunk and co-founder of the privacy blockchain Zcash. I had long since pieced together that this was the fairy-winged man I had met in Prague, still bewildered by his insistence on anonymity, even though I had easily looked up his real name on his Wikipedia page (Wikipedia, 2025).

In reward for our interest and attention at the meetup that night, each attendee was invited to share a cryptocurrency wallet address to be 'airdropped' a small amount of Zcash privacy coin to our digital wallet for free. To receive the equivalent of 18 cents in the privacy coin, I chose the Zcash mobile wallet brand called 'Nighthawk'. The transaction sent by Zooko included a secret memo containing a 'shielded love note', which was a message from the sender to the receiver that was cryptographically hidden from external surveillance or snooping. I was late to provide my wallet address to register for the airdrop, somewhat desperately 'DMing' (direct messaging) the well-known founder on Twitter in the middle of their talk to please include me in their software script that would drop to all the addresses at once.

'Hi! *wave emoji*. Please add me to your bash script. Wallet address: zs1tegqkd6ll92ktc2gxr874ljy7qjau5aa7pspp6rrktnaeyl82fgrdh6zxlr5pjznsdgpjmyqaef'.[5]

'Ty! *thank you hands emoji*'.

'Also, I would love to interview you for a research article on the cypherpunks and origins of decentralised technologies to test some assumptions', I stated.

To my surprise, they responded. 'Hi. Check your Shielded Love Notes!'

Opening up my Nighthawk wallet, the transaction memo read: 'Hi, Kelsie, nice to meet you! How did you think the meetup went? What assumptions are you trying to test?'.

With the tiny amount of coin I had received, I could still afford to send microtransactions of cryptocurrency with a memo attached each time. Each message exchanged was shielded by 'zero knowledge'[6] cryptography on the Zcash privacy coin blockchain. And via this most unusual blockchain-based interaction is how the ethics approval request to begin the research interview began.

Cryptography, and the privacy controls it affords people in digital domains, is the ideological, historical, technical and social foundation of decentralised technologies. The anonymous handle on Telegram, and the later insistence on communicating via Zcash, was all part of making decentralised technologies an identity and a lifestyle. This was one of many paradoxical experiences that would illuminate the principles and practicalities of the field of decentralised technologies, as well as an early lesson for me that security is at the core of decentralised technologies. The remainder of this chapter explores the foundational principles of decentralised security, beginning with an examination of key cryptographic building blocks.

Cryptography as the foundation of decentralised security

Security in decentralised technology communities is fundamentally rooted in cryptography. Cryptography is a tool for communication between two intended parties and no one else – it protects information by converting it into a coded format that only authorised parties can read by having the correct key to decode it. Cryptography provides the mathematical and computational mechanisms that enable secure interactions between counterparties that don't know each other. This process coordinates interactions among distributed participants and ensures the integrity of the blockchain record of transactions. In other words, cryptography offers 'secure communication via insecure channels' (Merkle, 1978). This type of encryption is a core technology for digital interactions and internet security because it provides essential protections for data against unwanted third-party access (Monsees, 2020). The use of encryption security to avoid external snooping informs the development of numerous open-source, peer-to-peer, encrypted decentralised technologies today.

In a technical sense, decentralisation in digital technologies refers to the typology of a distributed computational system. That is, decentralised technology systems, such as public blockchains, are a subset of distributed systems where multiple authorities control different components, and no authority is fully trusted by all (Troncoso *et al.*, 2017). Thus, decentralised systems represent a paradigm shift in how security is conceptualised and implemented, moving away from reliance on trusted, centralised intermediaries to cryptographic assurances embedded in the technical rules of software protocols and consensus mechanisms.[7]

While encryption is a cornerstone of digital privacy, it is also a site of contestation (Monsees, 2020). It shapes and is shaped by struggles for privacy, digital rights and democracy. At its core, encryption empowers individuals and communities by providing a means to communicate securely – meaning free from surveillance or censorship. This makes it a crucial tool for groups who rely on encrypted messaging and data protection to self-organise and resist unwanted external influences.

The argument is that governments and corporations often seek to limit or control encryption, citing that strong encryption can shield criminal activities or pose national security risks. This has led to ongoing debates between digital rights advocates and policymakers, reflecting broader tensions between state power and individual rights and autonomy. The tension also extends to corporate interests, as big tech firms are often left with the responsibility to balance user privacy with government demands for data access. Thus, the ability to encrypt one's data is not just a technical privilege but a fundamental aspect of digital rights, shaping the future of privacy, surveillance and political resistance.

Cryptographic security in decentralised technologies is deeply influenced by the ideological foundations from which these systems emerged. Decentralised security is not limited to technical measures; it also encompasses the governance structures and economic incentives that sustain these networks. The interaction between code, community and cryptography gives rise to the distinct security properties of decentralised infrastructures, shaping everything from blockchain consensus mechanisms to coordinated cybersecurity efforts. Understanding the history of encryption and security in these systems requires attention to both their technical components and the political and ideological dynamics that inform them. The following historical context provides a foundational understanding of the technical and ideological concepts underpinning decentralised technologies and their communities today, with particular attention to blockchain technology and its ideological underpinnings.

The origins of distributed computer networking

Distributed computing as a physical architecture for computer networks originated in the 1960s. It emerged from a US government project to maintain the availability of government and military communications infrastructure – developed against the existential threat of foreign nation-state nuclear attacks during the Cold War (IFTF, 2010). During this period, Paul Baran, a military engineer employed by the US government-funded research and development think tank 'RAND Corporation' authored thirteen papers on the topic of distributed communications (Rand Corporation, n.d.). The fundamental concept of Baran's decentralised communications infrastructure is the physical distribution of computing hardware and connecting all nodes in a network to each other via multiple links to make a system survivable against physical attack (Yoo, 2018). Baran explains that centralised networks are vulnerable, as the destruction of the central point of control destroys all communications across the network (Baran, 1964). Instead, he turned to the hopes of building communications networks that are as distributed as possible (Baran, 1964).

Engineers since Baran have adopted this approach of accommodating for the failure of critical components in systems through 'redundancy', meaning that if one part fails, another could take its place (Pierce, 1965). Baran also emphasised individual and collective data security via cryptography in the age of computers and the responsibility of the engineer for ensuring resilience (Abbate, 1999). This approach also informs the design of public, decentralised blockchain networks (Lamport *et al.*, 1982).

The influence of Baran's ideas continued as he mentored Lawrence Roberts in the development of the Advanced Research Projects Agency Network (ARPANET), the predecessor to the modern-day internet. Roberts argues that distributed computing was never just for the military, but for 'the entire world' (Bay, 2019: 76). Yet, Roberts was not concerned with the threat of the Cold War or 'survivability'. Thus, the principle of non-hierarchical distributed networking was not strictly adopted in ARPANET or the later internet, which instead emphasised data packets transmitted between two points in computer networking (known as packet flows) (Abbate, 1999).

Cryptography also featured as part of ARPANET's design in the cybersecurity device that operated between network switches and host computers (Dupont and Fidler, 2016) and National Science Foundation Network (NSFNET) which served as the internet's backbone in the 1980s and 1990s (Abbate, 2010). Tim Berners-Lee and others carried forward the idea of universal 'read-write' computing with the invention of the 'World Wide Web'. However, visions for these networks to evolve into an open, decentralised internet did not come to fruition. Instead, NSFNET was handed off to the private sector (Abbate, 2010), and privatisation led to the commercialisation and centralisation of power through data monetisation and surveillance (Abbate, 1999; Tarnoff, 2022).

1960s: culture hacking

Computing was not just part of the military-industrial complex or broader consumption but a culture of 'digital utopianism'. I thought almost eighty-year-old Stewart Brand, founder of the 1960s countercultural magazine the *Whole Earth Catalogue*, was an odd choice of keynote speaker to address thousands of mostly twenty-something-year-olds at the annual Ethereum developer conference ('DevCon') I attended in Prague in 2018 (Ethereum Foundation, 2018). He shuffled slowly through the hallways and sat observantly in the back of workshops on the latest research in blockchains, privacy and civilisation. His presence made more sense during his keynote presentation when he described his life's work as 'hacking civilisation', expressing his enthusiasm at the energy of the public blockchain community as the next revolution in personal computing. 'Infinite players look forward, not to a victory…but towards ongoing play', he stated, quoting philosopher James Carse on 'Finite and Infinite Games' (Carse, 1986: 18). It was then that

I understood the importance of cultural identity and ideology in shaping socio-technical movements.

The hacker movement

The origins of the subcultural hacker movement in the 1960s have been traced back to ideals of openness, decentralisation and creative experimentation (Turner, 2008), producing a fertile milieu for creative expression through technology. Emerging from institutions like MIT's Artificial Intelligence Lab and the Homebrew Computer Club in Silicon Valley, hackers in this period viewed computers not as tools of corporate or state control, but as instruments of personal empowerment and social transformation (Rankin, 2018). Brand famously declared that 'information wants to be free', a phrase that came to encapsulate the hacker ethos of sharing knowledge, dismantling hierarchies and fostering collective innovation.

Influenced by countercultural values and systems thinking, the hacker culture of the 1960s combined a hands-on approach to programming with utopian aspirations for reshaping society through technology. This narrative of hackers not as criminals or misfits but as pioneering architects of the digital frontier has helped lay the foundations for future open-source and internet-based community cultures that followed (Levy, 2010). Whether or not these historical representations accurately reflect the access and interactions of computer operators at the time, they have nevertheless shaped enduring narratives of hackers as playfully irreverent technical geniuses that continue to influence hacker culture today.

1970s–80s: public key cryptography for 'secure communications', and secure digital markets

Building on the ideals of 1960s hacker culture, the 1970s saw the emergence of publicly available public key cryptography as a critical innovation for enabling secure digital communication and exchange. Public key cryptography lets people communicate securely and verify identity across open networks. It is a foundational concept in digital security where two mathematically linked 'keys' (sequences of alphabetic letters) form a public key and a private key that are used for encryption, decryption and authentication between a sender and an intended receiver.

Security research in the 1970s was largely the domain of government defence force agencies and private corporations, such as IBM. Public key cryptography was independently discovered by government security agency cryptography researchers at the UK Government Communications Headquarters (GCHQ) in 1973, and by independent cryptography researchers Whitfield Diffie, Martin Hellman and Ralph Merkle in 1976. Cryptographers at the GCHQ created a high-level classified encryption scheme, called 'non-secret encryption', and eventually shared it with the National Security Agency (NSA) in the US (Williamson, 1974; Bamford, 1983). Because encryption was seen as a national security tool, research on and access to encryption technologies was highly embargoed. The NSA, for example, monitored all patent requests regarding cryptography and would legally classify any cryptography patents it deemed too powerful for the public (Yost, 2015a; Levy, 2002). In 1975, the US government also introduced the Data Encryption Standard, a national encryption standard for public and commercial use. However, the Data Encryption Standard was weaker than the independent cryptographers recommended for e-commerce and the individual use desired.[8]

Characters such as Whitfield Diffie and Martin Hellman, and later Ronald Rivest, Adi Shamir, Leonard Adleman and others, developed cryptographic protocols that allowed parties to communicate securely over open networks without prior shared secrets (Diffie and Hellman, 1976; Rivest *et al.*, 1978; Yost, 2015a; Yost, 2015b). These researchers feared for their lives due to hitting a 'hornet's nest' within the NSA's efforts to discourage academic work in the field and the Department of Commerce's encryption export restrictions (under the International Traffic in Arms Regulations, or ITAR) (Yost, 2015a: 32). Yet, their work marked a fundamental shift in the possibilities for general-purpose digital interactions, introducing the technical foundation for authentication, confidentiality and digital commerce.

In the 1980s, visionary projects such as Ted Nelson's Xanadu and Phil Salin's AMiX extended these cryptographic insights into speculative architectures for digital markets. Xanadu envisioned a universal hypertext system with embedded micropayments and version control, anticipating a future where authors could be compensated for information flows (Nelson, 1974; Drexler, 1991; Nelson, 1999). Meanwhile, AMiX sought to create an online marketplace for the exchange of information and services, relying on cryptographically secured contracts and mechanisms to prove reputation (Miller and Drexler, 1988; Lavoie, 1990; Lavoie *et al.*, 1990). These eclectic and visionary communities understood that economic activity in digital environments would require not just connectivity, but trust – secured by cryptographic systems that could support ownership, authentication and transactional integrity. Together, these efforts laid early conceptual and technical groundwork for the emergence of secure digital platform economies.

Crypto-politics

Cryptography carries with it infrastructural politics, imaginaries and possibilities at the intersection of personal and nation-state security. The mathematical capability to conceal communications exerts transformational controls over access to information. Social and political debates over access to encryption reflect a broader societal struggle over information asymmetries between governments, corporates and citizens (Zuboff, 2015). The politics of encryption technologies is a tool that different stakeholders apply to enact their vision of secure communications, whether that be a state or an individual. These politics surface in the technologies that integrate the capabilities of encryption. The public key cryptographers, including a number of individuals who later appear on the Cypherpunks Mailing List (and some that don't, notably David Chaum),[9] were deeply engaged in efforts to influence and shape policy debates for the collective purposes of individual and commercial security in the digital era. However, it is the Cypherpunks that introduced a political theory of decentralisation to create secure, decentralised digital infrastructures for individual autonomy from state surveillance.

1990s: from cryptographers to Cypherpunks and crypto-anarchy

In the 1990s, the Cypherpunk movement emerged as a radical extension of cryptographic and hacker cultures, advancing a political vision of privacy, autonomy and freedom through the use of strong encryption. Centred around figures such as Timothy C. May, Eric Hughes and John Gilmore, the Cypherpunks formed a loose but influential network of technologists committed to building decentralised digital infrastructures resistant to surveillance and centralised control (Nabben, 2023a). Bonding over a shared interest in the study and development of secure communication techniques, Hughes, May and Gilmore co-founded the Cypherpunks Mailing List in September 1992, hoping to create a space where privacy enthusiasts could talk about and develop anonymous online networks, politics and philosophy.

Throughout the 1990s, when the Mailing List formed and meetups occurred, the Cypherpunks were a relatively unimportant group that operated in their corner of the internet among numerous other hacker subcultures that were conducting infrastructural experimentations in peer-to-peer systems, encryption technologies and rulebreaking. This included peer-to-peer file-sharing systems such as 'BitTorrent', 'Pirate Bay' and others (McKelvey, 2018). Although it was little more than a passion project, reaching seven hundred members and around thirty messages a day at its peak, this early digital community would end up having an outsized influence on the world of crypto as we know it (Gilmore, 1999). The objectives of the Cypherpunks, according to the threads found on the Mailing List, were unregulated access to encryption, anonymous communications, cryptocurrencies and the development of platforms to constrain government power (Jarvis, 2021).

The Cypherpunks Mailings List led to various other publications that not only expanded Cypherpunk ideology, but laid the foundation for 'crypto-anarchy'. For example, Hughes's *A Cypherpunk Manifesto* (1993: n.p.) famously declared that 'privacy is necessary for an open society in the electronic age', emphasising the role of cryptography as a tool of individual empowerment and resistance. Fellow Cypherpunk Timothy May not only envisioned decentralised computer networking as a tool for the good of society, but wanted to re-shape the social, economic and political order to an extreme. May overlayed his political values onto the idea of digital cash to realise a vision of 'unstoppable' cryptographically enabled decentralised networks as tools for 'crypto-anarchy' against the state (May, 1992a). His call-to-arms expressed a view of cryptography and decentralisation as weapons against government surveillance and for establishing a 'libertaria' of post-government territories in cyberspace (May, 1992b).

Clearly, while World Wide Web developers had promised universal online self-expression through 'read-write' functionalities, Cypherpunks asserted these engineers failed to deliver on such individual freedoms. Later, in 2012, Wikileaks founder Julian Assange wrote, 'The internet, our greatest tool of emancipation, has been transformed into the most dangerous facilitator of totalitarianism we have ever seen' (Assange, 2012: 7). Deeper, more structural tools for societal change were needed. According to the Cypherpunks, anonymous digital cash was one such tool which could facilitate change by offering a means of disintermediated, digital self-coordination.

Contrary to the interests of the military-industrial complex at RAND Corporation, the Cypherpunks emerged out of the hacker and hippie culture in protest of the increasing capability of the state to monitor its citizens through digital networks. Informed by libertarian, anarchist and techno-utopian currents, Cypherpunks believed that code could substitute for law (Miller, 2017),[10] and that digital systems should be architected to ensure confidentiality, anonymity and censorship resistance by default. Their work reframed cryptography not merely as a security measure, but as a foundation for building sovereign systems that could operate outside the purview of traditional state or corporate oversight, enabling new forms of freedom in an increasingly digitised world.

Through their mailing list, along with prototypes and white papers, the Cypherpunk community laid the intellectual and technical groundwork for later developments in digital cash, anonymous remailers and ultimately public blockchain-based systems like Bitcoin – a peer-to-peer electronic cash representing the first public, permissionless and cryptographically secure cryptocurrency (Nakamoto, 2008).

Bitcoin: a decentralised technology for political decentralisation

These successive cultural eras – spanning the experimental hacker ethos of the 1960s, the cryptographic breakthroughs and market imaginaries of the 1970s and 1980s and the radical privacy politics of the 1990s Cypherpunks – culminated in the creation and launch of Bitcoin in 2009 as the first fully functional public, permissionless, cryptographically secure peer-to-peer public blockchain protocol. As a manifestation of decades of technical development and ideological utopianism, Bitcoin is both a technological artefact and a political statement. It has been described as a 'theory of the larger social order (or a challenge to it)' (Swartz, 2018: 623).

As a decentralised digital currency, Bitcoin integrates public key cryptography, peer-to-peer networking and a novel distributed consensus mechanism – Proof of Work – to establish a trustless system of value exchange without central intermediaries. It was anonymously founded and remains an independent, collectively governed, technologically and politically decentralised and cryptographically secure digital infrastructure. Many technical hacker, open-source, computer engineer, Cypherpunk innovations led to Bitcoin's emergence (Nakamoto, n.d.).

Bitcoin also embodied the Cypherpunks' core political aim, which according to list contributor (and later founder of privacy blockchain 'Zcash', also known as 'Martin' in the opening anecdote) Zooko Wilcox was 'self-governance through technological means' (Foresight Institute, 2022). Bitcoin is a response to the vision of 'computer security as the future of law' by Mark Miller and other Cypherpunks for a protocol that can provide cryptographically guaranteed execution of agreements.

More than a financial instrument, Bitcoin crystallises a broader infrastructural milieu: it embodies decentralisation not merely as a technical design, but as a contested and evolving social and political ideology. In this context, decentralisation becomes a political principle of governance, coordination and resistance, aimed at mitigating the risks of centralised power and fostering systems of distributed interaction, transaction and coordination. Public blockchains embody this ethos by enabling programmable, verifiable and transparent infrastructures for digital exchange. As such, Bitcoin and its successor blockchains contribute to a new paradigm of decentralised digital security – one in which the integrity of the system emerges from the distributed consensus of its participants, rather than from institutional oversight or coercive authority.

Bitcoin's incorporation of decentralised computing infrastructure and decentralisation of any single point of control inspired an explosion of innovation and development in distributed, open source, cryptographically secured decentralised technologies to follow in its ideology of political empowerment.

2009–present: cryptoeconomics and decentralised technologies

By 2015, the narrative had evolved from 'Bitcoin' to 'blockchain' (Swartz, 2017) (although Bitcoin, the original, 'immutable' public blockchain persists as the largest blockchain by market capitalisation, although not necessarily developer community). The second largest of these is the Ethereum public blockchain, which provides an infrastructural foundation for anyone to develop applications on (or software 'apps') according to their own purposes and threat models (Buterin, 2014).

In his late teens, the author for 'Bitcoin Magazine' and soon-to-be co-founder of the Ethereum blockchain, Vitalik Buterin, was clearly inspired by the Cypherpunks (Buterin, 2012). The counter-state political contribution of the Cypherpunks echoes throughout the Ethereum blockchain community today in the call to build a free and open digital economy and society (a.k.a. 'make Ethereum Cypherpunk again') (Buterin, 2023).

The guiding theoretical contribution from the Ethereum community is the idea of cryptoeconomics, which describes the multi-disciplinary approach that uses economic incentives and cryptography to guide new kinds of secure systems for societal coordination (Voskuil *et al.*, 2020; Voshmgir and Zargham, 2020; Nabben, 2023a). This concept was heavily informed by the Cypherpunks, who argued 'all cryptography is economics…Repeat after me. Cryptography is all economics' (Hughes, 1997: n.p.).

Co-founder of the Cypherpunks Mailing List, Eric Hughes, argues that cryptography provides security to users of a distributed system by making the cost of attack more expensive (Hughes, 1997). This is because when a cryptographic system is scaled, the attacker is forced to weigh up a higher cost of attack against the potential reward. This logic undergirds the consensus system of public blockchains. In other words, a decentralised network can be cheap to secure and expensive to attack through scale (as, to attack the consensus rules that govern the system, they need to buy 51 per cent of the entire supply of currency on a network), providing relative security for users through economic principles, or 'computation and markets' (Lavoie *et al.*, 1990).

Limitations of this hacky history

Of course, the ideological lineage presented, while I believe it authentically represents the views of decentralised technology proponents consulted during the research, is admittedly somewhat idealistic. It is important to acknowledge that alternative narratives about the values and history of Web3 exist – narratives that are far less favourable to the open-source, decentralised and emancipatory vision explored here. These include critiques concerning financialisation, technocracy and the environmental impacts of digitisation. While many of these concerns are beyond the scope of this book, they are thoroughly examined in other scholarly work. There is, however, an irony in presenting any lens through which to view the history of decentralised technologies: the early promises of Web2 were similarly optimistic and participatory, yet idealistic narrative framing ultimately masked the rise of extractive business models that went largely unchallenged until mainstream scandals brought them to light. One of the aims of this book is to address that risk in real time in relation to Web3 by focusing on the security challenges and practices shaping decentralised technologies today, and by highlighting strategies for addressing them.

Conclusion

In this historical arc, security is not an afterthought but a foundational prerequisite for the viability of digital economies. From the early ambitions of hacker collectives to democratise access to computing to the cryptographic infrastructures envisioned by Xanadu and AMiX, and the Cypherpunks' framing of privacy as political resistance, the consistent thread emerges that economic coordination in digital environments depends on robust mechanisms for ensuring integrity, confidentiality and authenticity. Public blockchains like Bitcoin extend this legacy by embedding security into the very architecture of digital exchange – replacing trust in institutions with trust in code, protocols and consensus mechanisms. In doing so, they establish a new security paradigm that is decentralised, adaptive and tightly coupled to economic value, yet also highly precarious and subject to its own threats and vulnerabilities. As digital economies continue to develop, security must be recognised not just as a technical concern, but as a fundamental social and political condition that shapes how value is created, exchanged and protected.

Now that we have traced the ideological lineage from which today's blockchain security practices have emerged, we turn in the coming chapters to examine their present manifestations. The next chapter outlines the current state of blockchain security, asking what it means for decentralised technologies to be considered 'secure' – and, crucially, from whom or what. This inquiry lays the foundation to move beyond abstract ideals to investigate how security is operationalised, negotiated and experienced across decentralised technology ecosystems today.

Notes

1 Intellectual histories outline the lineage and significance of key characters' ideas, actions and arguments in relation to security and decentralisation, as well as how these ideas have been transformed by various stakeholders over multiple decades (Whatmore, 2016).

2 The concept of 'infrastructural milieu' refers to the factors and conditions created around a technical object that help to sustain activities of production and circulation (Simondon, 2017). The associated milieu of infrastructure is not just the backdrop against which technological systems operate; it is the social, economic and cultural dimensions that interact to form an integral part of the system's operational logic, evolution and stabilisation (Bowker *et al.*, 2009).

3 Note: this is no longer my handle on Telegram, so don't try to contact me here.

4 Often referred to as 'the decentralised Web', Web3 refers to online platforms and applications based on public, decentralised blockchains that are user-owned, rather than controlled by third-party providers,

to allow users to 'read', 'write' and coordinate with others without intermediaries (Nabben, 2023a). The term was coined by co-founder of the Ethereum blockchain, Gavin Wood, and gained popularity among cryptocurrency communities and venture capitalists to describe a new wave of innovation (Edelman, 2021), including public blockchains, Decentralised Autonomous Organisations (DAOs), Non-Fungible Tokens (NFTs) and metaverses. 'Web3' has also become a marketing term to attract a new wave of venture capital towards certain technical innovations (Sadowski and Beegle, 2023; Faustino, 2023).

5 Note: not my actual wallet address.

6 Zero-knowledge cryptography allows someone to prove they know something (like a password, secret key or solution to a problem) without revealing the details of what that something is. More specifically, a zero-knowledge proof (ZKP) is a method in cryptography that allows one party (the *prover*) to prove to another party (the *verifier*) that a statement is true without revealing any information beyond the truth of the statement itself.

7 The standardised rules and incentives of a software protocol that allow distributed 'nodes' in the network to communicate and agree on the validity and order of events (known as the 'state').

8 A government attempt to control encryption standards by publishing an approved encryption standard for public and commercial use. This attempt to regulate and limit citizens' access to cryptography knowledge and tools was just one event in a series in the contestation of cryptography and security, and the decades-long battle over data privacy known as the 'Crypto Wars'. See: Landau, 2000; Jarvis, 2020; Levy, 2002; Electronic Frontier Foundation, 2014.

9 One of the most influential cryptography academics and forefathers of electronic currencies. Although Chaum did not associate himself with the Cypherpunks, his work inspired further research into privacy-preserving, decentralised, digital currencies.

10 This is illustrated in a thesis titled 'Computer Security as the Future of Law' by Mark Miller (Miller, 2017), who appears numerous times in the Cypherpunk Mailing List Archives (Miller, n.d.).

2

The state of blockchain security

Introduction

This chapter examines the current state of blockchain security – or more accurately, persistent insecurity. Despite ideological commitments to cryptographic guarantees and protocol-level integrity from project founders, blockchain systems remain vulnerable. Security is not guaranteed by design but is continuously negotiated by a patchwork of stakeholders. Drawing on ethnographic analysis of security incidents as well as publicly available data on high-profile exploits, this chapter maps key attack vectors, threat actors and stakeholders. It presents a matrix of the decentralised security ecosystem, characterised as much by fragmentation and improvisation as by technical sophistication. This ecosystem has evolved to include software auditors, bug bounty hunters, protocol security teams, white hat hackers, user education initiatives, insurance providers, policymakers and more. These stakeholders operate according to various incentives and an ethos of decentralisation that complicates traditional notions of responsibility, liability and enforcement across protocols, projects and users.

This chapter argues that decentralised digital infrastructure is insecure by default. While this is true of digital infrastructure more broadly, what sets this ecosystem apart is its explicit recognition of that condition, and by extension, the strategies created to co-exist with it. Insecurity is not a flaw to be resolved; it is a constitutive feature of how decentralised systems are built, governed and experienced. The challenge for developers and users of decentralised technologies, then, is not to eliminate all vulnerabilities, but to understand how a diverse set of actors can navigate, negotiate and coordinate within a landscape of ever-evolving threats (from hackers to nation-state adversaries, and more – as will be detailed in the chapters that follow).

Threats are a phone call away

It was a sunny mid-morning at my friend's house, where I had gone to visit during my lunch break. The pulled beef sandwiches were toasting when my phone rang. It was an unknown number, but I figured I would answer anyway (this was my first mistake, and thankfully, my only one on this occasion).

Given it was an unknown caller, I answered the phone with a brief 'Hello?'

'Hello, Kelsie [Surname – not my academic pseudonym that I use professionally but my married name]', stated a man with a smooth British accent. 'This is Clive from the Ledger cryptocurrency hardware wallet[1] security team. Do you have a moment to speak?'

A sick feeling emerged from my stomach all the way up to my head and down to my toes. 'You've got to be kidding me', I snapped, and hung up the phone.

In previous times when an obvious phishing scam had come my way, such as a message on the chat application Telegram from a contact asking to borrow some cryptocurrency, I had the self-discipline to string them along to better understand their tactics. This typically included finding out their wallet address (almost always clean), and notifying the actual contact via a different channel that they were being impersonated. But not this time. The intrusion of my personal space on a lazy day off had caught me off guard.

Unsure how they had my married name, my phone number and presumably knew I had something to do with cryptocurrency (although, somewhat unfortunately, I only hold a nominal amount for research purposes), the invasiveness of the call left me with that queasy feeling for the rest of the day. If this was my reality as a 'no one' to the broader crypto industry, who knows what security threats high-profile crypto-founders, team members and other contributors were experiencing.

Insecure by default

Decentralised network architectures present unique security affordances, as well as unique challenges due to their structural and cultural characteristics. The permissionless nature of blockchain technology means that anyone can participate in the use, development and governance of a project by adhering to pre-specified rules, without requiring permission from a central authority (Nabben and Zargham, 2022). The open-source software culture also means that anyone can launch a cryptocurrency project, and people can (in theory – if they have the technical skills) audit the code themselves and choose whether to use it or not. Furthermore, the nature of open source is that everyone assumes that someone else is working on security. However, these qualities complicate quality control of software code and system design, as well as incident response. Unlike other digital systems, decentralised infrastructures are built with explicit recognition that digital domains are insecure by default – from the infrastructure to any dependencies on other software and hardware, to user practices, you are responsible. Thus, rather than assuming security as a baseline, these systems are designed with the understanding that exposure to risk is inherent and must be continuously managed through distributed mechanisms.

The nature of the threat

The current state of blockchain security does not reflect a domain of digital security. Known for high-profile hacks, scams and links to funding North Korea's nuclear weapons programme, the industry faces serious questions of legitimacy – not only from end-users and policymakers, but often from within its own ecosystem.

The 2022 report of Web3 hacks and vulnerabilities by bug bounty platform 'Immunefi' states that 'Infrastructure is King. In 2022, 46.5 per cent of all hacks occurred via infrastructure' (Immunefi, 2022: 5). At this time, one of the biggest security issues was private key management, which is essential in a decentralised context whereby users are responsible for the custody of their own assets. Since 2022, security concerns have evolved to include phishing scams, social engineering of blockchain project employees to gain access and the professionalisation of crypto theft.

Frauds, scams and rug pulls: crypto hack stats

The global market capitalisation of cryptocurrencies surpassed US $3 trillion in 2024. Over $137 billion of this is in Decentralised Finance (DeFi) protocols (known as Total Value Locked or TVL). In 2024, there were over 232 known instances of hacking exploits and fraud instances, totalling almost $1.5 billion lost (Immunefi, 2024: 3). A staggering $540 million of this was stolen across just two hacks (a Japanese crypto exchange called DMM Bitcoin and an Indian exchange called WazirX) (Immunefi, 2024: 4). While most attacks were directed at DeFi protocols, CeFi (centralised finance outlets, such as centralised cryptocurrency exchanges) sustained the biggest losses.

Hacks differ by blockchain. Ethereum, in which the majority of this research took place, is the most targeted chain, with crypto hackers stealing $572 million in the second quarter of 2024 (a 112 per cent increase from the previous year).

The nature of the threat is serious. Two significant attacks that cleared $285 million in funds in 2024 were a major exchange in India called WazirX and a decentralised lending and borrowing protocol called Radiant Capital. Security researchers have pointed out the similarities in techniques between the two attacks, emphasising that both were carried out by well-resourced North Korean state-backed hackers (more on this later and in Chapter 6) (Gupta, 2024; Von Fange, 2024).

The Security Alliance (SEAL) convenes a number of online chat forums for protocol founders, security leads, white hat hackers and security service providers across Web3 to share knowledge and organise responses to security news, trends and incidences.[2] Conversations in the main general chat channel are telling of the state of security in the blockchain industry (as of early 2024).

> I think we have a long way to go as an industry. We severely lack fundamentals and Web3 organizations rarely think beyond the network…even just basic personal security fundamentals and opsec

> [operational security], carrying keys around, leaving devices unattended, etc. In this space of remote and decentralized work contribution from a beautifully uncontrolled environment we do not focus on what that means to organizational security posture. Sharing intelligence is certainly a part of the equation, but I don't think we've truly decided how to act on intelligence in a coordinated way – I really hope to get that out of this group. (Private communication, SEAL chat)[3]

In another thread, one white hat (a.k.a. 'for good') hacker shared:

> I was helping a blockchain protocol last night and they were highly unprepared for it on the Web2 side, no logs configured, not sure about IAM roles, not sure what was open on the net or how creds are kept, no environment safety net for gh [GitHub] secrets, etc. Its super boring but I think a 'sensible security' guide for Web2 assets for web3 companies might be a good idea.

Ryan Wegner, former lead of SEAL intelligence ('intel') initiative, remarked in a research interview that the state of blockchain security

> varies a lot from project to project. It seems poor because it's easy to find the projects that aren't doing well because they lack basic security processes and practices and these mistakes are public on the blockchain for everyone to see [...] Because the bar is so low to actually deploy a project, they don't think about security until much further down the track. Unlike Web2, Web3 startups are often responsible for protecting millions in TVL of retail funds, and security professionals are forced to reverse engineer products in production to retroactively apply security best practices...like adding seat belts to a plane that's already in flight. (ethnographic interview)

This was echoed in a research interview with Security Researcher and SEAL contributor Craig ('x86NOP'), who stated: 'There is an intense pressure to innovate and ship functionality at a pace that isn't conducive to learning best practices or the many tools available to properly secure the systems upon which web3 is built' (ethnographic interview). This results in engineers who are experts in cryptocurrency technology but fail to acknowledge the trade-offs of decentralised architecture and security, leading to routine exploits.

In an earlier effort to help projects improve their security posture in the blockchain industry, security researchers have developed resources, such as the 'Rekt Test' questionnaire (Immunefi, 2023), as a simple and widely applicable evaluation to help projects ensure at least a minimum level of security controls. While many of these basic security measures are simple to implement, they are not always practised in a startup culture that prioritises building and deploying software. Furthermore, exploits are not only occurring and addressable at the level of protocol security. The many types of exploits occurring include social engineering tactics, such as phishing scams, 'pig butchering' attacks, SIM swapping and more, as detailed in the sections that follow.

People acknowledge that the state of blockchain security is lacking, both for individual users and as a collective. In one example, it took one blockchain project team *six days* to realise that *$600 million in cryptocurrency tokens* was missing amidst the largest crypto hack at the time in 2021. When the Ronin bridge[4] (a 'side chain' infrastructure designed to support high-throughput low-fee transactions for gaming applications) team eventually did realise, they announced: 'We discovered the attack this morning after a report from a user being unable to withdraw 5,000 ETH from the bridge' (Rekt News, n.d.a; Ronin, 2022). Only after this announcement did they realise that the bridge had been hacked an entire week earlier. 'The bar is pretty low tbh' (to be honest), stated one SEAL in reference to the incident. Others in the chat reacted with a vomiting face and rolling on the floor laughing emojis, reinforcing how absurd it was.

The Ronin Hack incident highlighted the security trade-offs of centralised points of failure within ostensibly decentralised infrastructures. Attackers compromised validator nodes to steal approximately $625 million of value in the Ethereum network's ETH token and USDC stable coins. The breach was linked to a social engineering attack and weak validator decentralisation (there were only nine validator nodes at the time, with five needing to be compromised for control).

Individually, it is an extremely common occurrence for participants in this industry to suffer losses of assets. For example, the website 'Scam Sniffer' that provides regular security updates shared a regular-style post on their X account, stating: '43 mins ago, someone lost 12,083 spWETH ($32.43M) after signing a "permit" phishing signature' (Scam Sniffer, 2024). According to the Internet Crime Complaint Center Cryptocurrency Fraud Report, the number of cryptocurrency-related complaints represents about 10 per cent of the total number of financial fraud complaints, yet the losses associated with these complaints account for almost 50 per cent of the total losses of online fraud (IC3, 2023, 3). As one SEAL in the chat states, 'It makes me so mad we [the blockchain ecosystem] aren't doing better'.

Web2 security versus Web3 security

Blockchain developers are not only developing an industry from the ground up, but also the security infrastructure and tooling to service it. Traditional digital network security is oriented around delegated stakeholder responsibilities for protecting centralised structures with clear boundaries. Alternatively, cybersecurity in blockchain-based networks deals with the unique challenges of navigating decentralised networks and complex ecosystems. Decentralised security involves distribution of network data across nodes to operate a protocol and enhance network resilience. Security in this context also includes individual responsibility for managing cryptographic keys, ensuring the security of smart contracts, systemic risk of cascade failure across both technology and cryptocurrency token prices and more. Moreover, participation in blockchain systems can involve security risks stemming from their decentralised and permissionless features, such as the irreversibility of transactions, the ability for anyone to deploy code within low bureaucracy start-up culture and the absence of a central authority to provide recourse when problems occur.

Another illustration of the precarious state of blockchain security is demonstrated in a strange unfolding of events in June 2024 between blockchain security auditing firm Certik and well-known cryptocurrency exchange Kraken. Certik allegedly stole $3 million in funds by exploiting a bug in Kraken. Yet, instead of responsibly reporting the bug via Kraken's bug bounty programme (that provides financial incentives for responsible disclosure), Certik claimed that their actions were in the name of 'white hat' (for good) hacking, to aid Kraken by publicly revealing their security vulnerabilities. Meanwhile, Kraken is treating it as a criminal case of unauthorised access, and pursuing legal recourse (AndrewMohawk, 2024).

Kraken Chief Security Officer, Nicholas Percoco, stated: 'In the essence of transparency, we are disclosing this bug to the industry today. We are being accused of being unreasonable and unprofessional for requesting that "white-hat hackers" return what they stole from us. Unbelievable' (Percoco, 2024). In other words, Certik's behaviour was abnormal by security industry standards because they exploited the bug instead of responsibly disclosing it to the organisation in private (which is often rewarded retrospectively at the organisation's discretion, or formally pre-advertised as a bug bounty reward).

Blockchain security practitioners were outraged by this conduct, asserting that Certik's actions undermined trust in crypto security actors (especially white hats) and put users at risk. Security experts issued public statements to slam the poor behaviour: for example, Andrew MacPherson (AndrewMohawk), Principal Security Engineer at Privy and SEAL Technical Council member, stated, 'Ethical hacking means you report vulnerabilities immediately to prevent exploitation and help the community'. More sharply, Samczsun, SEAL Founder/CEO, stated: 'stop fucking it up for the rest of us' (referring to white hat hacking and bug bounty programmes). Although what it means to be a blockchain white hat hacker remains uncodified, there are norms around codes of conduct, alignment of interests and incentives.

Security stakeholders

Blockchain industry stakeholders operate according to varying incentives, from bug bounty hunters that receive pre-agreed platform rewards upon success, to white hats who act based on moral conviction and hope that they will be compensated after successfully intervening in an incident (see Table 2.4: Blockchain security actor incentive landscape). This unique typology of stakeholders highlights that blockchain security is governed not by a single model of incentive alignment but by a plurality of moral stances and legitimacy claims. In decentralised systems, where formal enforcement outside of protocol-encoded rules is weak, the distinctions between civic duty, contractual obligation, mercenary service and opportunistic exploitation become blurred. In this context, security responses are structured by varied economic and moral incentives. Legitimacy claims (such as stewardship, a moral obligation to community duty or contractual compliance) are as important as technical capability in determining which actors are trusted, invited into crisis response war rooms or volunteer teams, and compensated for their contributions.

Threat actors

The blockchain security threat landscape consists of an array of attacks, hacks and scams that target different layers of blockchain ecosystems and participants. These threats exploit vulnerabilities in protocol design, smart contracts, infrastructure, and consensus mechanisms, as well as human behaviours (known as 'social engineering').

Peter Kacherginsky, security researcher at major exchange Coinbase and editor of the *Blockthreat Intelligence* newsletter, describes the DeFi threat landscape as shifting across 2022–24 from smart contract exploits to price oracle manipulation, to private key compromises and malicious insider attacks (DeFi Security Summit, 2024c: at 5:25). He breaks down DeFi threat actors into four categories:

1. 'Cryptonatives' (i.e. 'one of us' – financially and ego-motivated individuals with strong software development and security capabilities),
2. Criminal Advanced Persistent Threats (APTs; financially motivated criminal organisations proficient at evading law enforcement and money laundering),
3. Nation State APTs (state-sponsored actors tasked and resourced for asset acquisition), and
4. Malicious insiders (trusted insiders, such as technical team members, abusing their legitimate access for gain) (DeFi Security Summit, 2024a: at 5:25).

Other threat actor categories that surfaced throughout my research include 'script kiddies' – amateur attackers that engage in opportunistic exploits (involving both scams or physical violence for ransom money), and automated bots[5] which play a key role in front-running (see Maximal Extractable Value [MEV] below), spam attacks (see Sybil below) and brute-force attempts (see Distributed Denial of Service [DDoS] below).

Tactics, techniques and procedures

Cryptocurrency attacks can be organised into two major categories: (i) fraud (such as scams or 'rug pulls', whereby people invest in a token and the value is tanked via withdrawals or abandonment of the project, leaving them with a worthless asset), and (ii) hacks (or attacks, whereby there is a failure in the design of the smart contract, poor implementation or an infrastructural weakness) (Immunefi, 2022).

Table 2.2: Blockchain security industry taxonomy shows a number of categories and examples of blockchain security vulnerabilities, loosely organised from the base-level logic of the protocol, up the technology stack to error or manipulation of human behaviour. Although not intended to be an exhaustive list, Table 2.2 provides an overview of the blockchain security landscape.

Security Researcher and SEAL contributor Craig ('x86NOP'), highlights that during his many years in the field, various types of vulnerabilities and attacks have been met with different levels of exploitation and emphasis from the crypto security industry (ethnographic interview). The major concerns used to be 51 per cent of attacks at the protocol level[6] and smart contract hacks. For example, the early days of Solidity (the main programming coding language for coding smart contracts on the Ethereum blockchain) had numerous, highly technical pitfalls. This made it difficult for every developer to fully understand them, creating an attack surface for sophisticated attackers to exploit protocols (especially DeFi) that implemented their contracts with anything less than perfection. In some cases, contracts were 'perfectly' implemented at the time of deployment, only for later discoveries of bugs in the underlying compilers that left their software vulnerable.

Table 2.1 Cryptocurrency exploits (by trend and timeframe)

Category	Active period	Example attacks
Exchange compromises	2014–25	Mt. Gox, Coincheck, Phemex, Bybit
Smart contract exploits	2016–present	The DAO, Parity, multiple DeFi hacks
Cross-chain bridge attacks	2021–present	Poly Network, Ronin
Flash loan/economic exploits	2020–present	bZx, Alpha, Yearn forks
Front-end and supply chain attacks	2023–present	Velodrome, Safe Wallet
Social engineering	2022–present	Lazarus phishing, Discord attacks
Governance exploits	2020–present	DAO vote manipulation
Consensus layer attacks	2018–20 (mostly)	Ethereum Classic 51%

Note: Table 2.1 presents a typology of security actors and their associated incentive structures, coordination tactics and legitimacy claims. These ideal types are intended as heuristic lenses: in practice, actors may shift between roles across incidents, and hybrid forms frequently emerge. The value of this typology lies not in static categorisation, but in highlighting the recurring moral economies and coordination dynamics that shape blockchain security responses.

Some of these commonplace issues have been mitigated by improvements in developer ('dev') skills to improve Ethereum's software code language (Solidity), code compilers and common software libraries (that make code components available for others to implement). Although, according to Craig, 'that's never to say any code is ever 100% safe and future gaps will surely arise' (ethnographic interview). The clear pattern is that once security professionals implement effective countermeasures that reduce the return-on-investment (ROI) for attackers and the low-hanging fruit in one category of attack vector are exhausted, threat actors shift their focus to a different category.

Meanwhile, some attack vectors – such as private key compromises and phishing – continue to be largely effective due to the prevalence of reactive defence measures and human errors. Below is a timeline highlighting notable incidents categorised by attack vectors, illustrating this progression (see Table 2.1: Cryptocurrency

Exploits (by trend and timeframe). Table 2.3: Cryptocurrency hack/attack trend timeline and Table 2.4: Chronological timeline of the largest blockchain hacks are listed at the end of this chapter.

Protocol-level attacks

Protocol-level attacks exploit vulnerabilities in the fundamental architecture of blockchain networks. These types of attacks are what the consensus layer of distributed blockchain networks aims to protect against. Among the most widely recognised threats to blockchain security is a 51% Attack, in which a single entity gains control of a majority of the network's hashing power (in Proof of Work systems) or staked tokens (in Proof of Stake systems), thereby compromising the integrity of the consensus mechanism that governs the operation of the blockchain. Such an attack would enable the attacker to corrupt the immutable record of transactions, including double-spending, censorship and chain reorganisation.

An example of a protocol-level attack is 'The Shanghai Attacks' against the Ethereum blockchain. In this occurrence, someone tried to attack the consensus algorithm of the entire network during the biannual developer conference in Shanghai, while the core team of Ethereum co-founders and developers convened in a panic in conference hallways to respond (DeFi Security Summit, 2025). Other attacks of this category include an eclipse attack, where a malicious entity isolates a target node by controlling all of its peer connections. This can be used to delay transactions, alter transaction orders or assist in double-spending exploits. Additionally, selfish mining is a strategy by cryptocurrency miners whereby they keep newly mined blocks private instead of broadcasting them to the network, centralising mining power and giving them an unfair advantage.

Cryptographic weaknesses

Weaknesses in cryptographic implementation are a lesser focus but a serious risk to blockchain security. One example of this is weak signature schemes, where flaws in digital signatures allow attackers to forge transactions or replay old ones. For example, the PlayDapp exploit in 2023 took advantage of signature vulnerabilities to conduct unauthorised transactions (Nefture Security, 2024).

Another more talked-about risk to cryptographic security is the impending development of quantum computing: a new paradigm of computing which uses the principles where information is processed in fundamentally different ways than classical computing. The risk of quantum computing is that it could be powerful enough to break the current encryption algorithms of public blockchains. In the long term, advances in quantum computing pose an existential threat to current cryptographic algorithms, necessitating advances in post-quantum cryptography towards the development of 'quantum-resistant' cryptographic protocols.

Smart contract exploits

A significant and persistent focus of the blockchain security industry is on smart contract hacks. Smart contract vulnerabilities present some of the most damaging technical security risks in the blockchain space, as well as the most audited by security service provider firms. One example of a common exploit in this class of attacks is the re-entrancy attack, where a contract makes an external call to another contract before updating its own 'state' (the present condition of the system), allowing attackers to repeatedly call the function to withdraw funds. An infamous example of this type of vulnerability is 'the DAO hack' in 2016, which led to a loss of around $55 million of value at the time in Ethereum network's ETH token – a PTSD-inducing memory for some white hat hackers that were involved in trying to rescue funds as the attack occurred. This particular case led to a high-profile community disagreement on whether or not a transaction history should be reversed and chain split (known as a 'hard fork' of the community operators and technical blockchain itself) between Ethereum and Ethereum classic (DuPont, 2017: 158).

Other examples of exploits related to smart contracts are access control vulnerabilities, logic errors in the software code or oracle manipulation attacks – where external data sources that feed information to the blockchain to inform events (oracles) are deliberately altered to deceive smart contracts, leading to incorrect pricing or liquidation events. Oracle manipulation attacks have been used to exploit major DeFi platforms. For example, the Synthetix DeFi protocol experienced an oracle exploit in 2019, whereby the arbitrage bot owner who unintentionally stole over $1 billion in native tokens agreed to reverse the trades for a bounty (Warwick, 2019).

Network and infrastructure attacks

Attacks targeting blockchain infrastructure and network operations can compromise decentralisation and security. Sybil attacks involve creating multiple fake identities to manipulate governance decisions, vote in decentralised protocols or spam networks. This type of attack targets systems where it pays to have multiple identities, such as the GitcoinDAO crowdfunding platform where all donated funds are matched by another pool of funds (Nabben, 2023b).

In DDoS attacks, adversaries flood blockchain nodes or the memory pool of transaction data ('mempools') at the network layer with excessive traffic or transactions, aiming to degrade performance, increase latency or halt consensus and service availability. A notable example of a DDoS attack was the Solana network congestion issues in 2022, where malicious actors exploited vulnerabilities to overload the system. Another severe threat is routing and web Domain Name Service (DNS) hijacking, where attackers manipulate blockchain communication by redirecting network traffic. This was demonstrated in the Ethereum Classic DNS hijack attack of 2019. Additionally, sidechain and bridge exploits have become a prime target, as these components often have weaker security measures than the main blockchain. The Ronin Bridge ($620 million) and Wormhole Bridge ($325 million) hacks exemplify the high-stakes vulnerabilities associated with cross-chain interoperability.

Economic attacks

DeFi protocols introduce new economic risks that attackers frequently exploit. Flash loan attacks have become particularly notorious, as they allow attackers to borrow large amounts of uncollateralised funds and manipulate price oracles to drain liquidity pools (a smart contract-based reserve of cryptocurrency tokens locked into a DeFi platform that enables users to trade, lend or borrow assets). One notable example of this is the Harvest Finance exploit in 2020, where approximately $24 million was stolen using flash loan manipulation.

Another critical issue is MEV attacks, where validators or front-runners reorder transactions for profit in accordance with the rules of the blockchain protocol but often at the expense of regular users. This is particularly problematic in sandwich attacks, where bots manipulate the execution order of trades. Additionally, liquidity 'rug pulls' are an economic scam in which project developers attract funds from investors and then remove all liquidity, vanishing with the capital. A famous case was the Squid Game Token rug pull in 2021, where the developers disappeared with around $3 million. Rug pulls reach new heights in every crypto hype cycle bubble, such as in 2024 when public identities and social media memes were leveraged to conduct such attacks.[7] Prime examples of rug pulls include the US President Donald Trump '$TRUMP' and First Lady '$MELANIA' meme coins in January 2025. The $TRUMP coin's value surged initially before declining sharply, with major holders profiting millions of dollars, despite substantial losses by other investors. The sharp volatility and insider profits raised concerns within the cryptocurrency community in relation to the legitimacy of the industry and risks to retail investors. Security Researcher Craig ('x86NOP') explained:

> These events showed clear manipulation by insiders and have been attributed to a sharp decline in 'meme coin' tokens normally very popular in this phase of a crypto bull run. It seems that the grifters[8] have developed sophisticated enough tools and cabals that rapid rise and fall token values that were once seen as fun gambles for speculators have been overrun by mechanisms virtually ensuring losses

where occasional wins by average people were once believed possible. (ethnographic interview)

Another prevalent issue is the rise of Ponzi and pyramid schemes masquerading as legitimate crypto projects. BitConnect was one of the most infamous early cases of this in 2018, defrauding investors of approximately $2 billion via charismatic marketing videos and influencer conferences before collapsing. These videos have since been edited into widely viewed memes that circulate in the living memory of crypto-communities.

Social engineering and operational security

Many blockchain attacks do not rely on technical exploits but instead manipulate human behaviour and operational security vulnerabilities, known as 'social engineering', to gain access to a system. Phishing attacks are among the most common, where malicious websites, emails, job offers, investor interest or fake web interfaces on Decentralised Applications (DApps) deceive users into revealing their private keys or seed phrases. According to some reports, these resulted in $494 million in losses in 2024 (Scam Sniffer, 2025). A well-known case was the Ledger phishing attacks following a data breach.

SIM swapping is another prevalent social engineering threat where attackers hijack a victim's phone number to reset account credentials and access crypto wallets. This has even happened to Vitalik Buterin, co-founder of the Ethereum blockchain, which resulted in his Twitter account being hacked. Another well-known example is the prominent crypto investor Michael Terpin, who suffered approximately $24 million in losses in a SIM swap attack and tried (unsuccessfully) to sue telecommunications provider AT&T for allowing hackers to bribe call centre workers to swap his phone SIM settings and redirect calls and messages to his phone number, so they could then compromise his accounts (United States District Court of California, 2019). The ruling was later overturned in court by an appeal against AT&T and in favour of Terpin.

Another example of a failing of traditional, centralised companies that resulted in Web3 hacks was regarding major US cryptocurrency exchange Coinbase. In this case, an overseas customer support worker in India was bribed for as little as a few hundred dollars to provide access to an estimated $400 million of customer information (Weiss and Roberts, 2025).

Insider threats are also significant, as developers or team members with privileged access can deliberately exploit projects for personal gain. This can be prevalent in a distributed, remote working culture, where developers can be hired and given access to systems without ever meeting other team members in person. Many rug pull scams have involved project insiders draining liquidity before abandoning their platforms. Another emerging issue is address poisoning, where attackers send small transactions from addresses that closely resemble a victim's legitimate contacts, tricking them into sending funds to the wrong address. Well-known examples of this occurred with 'vanity addresses', that could be reverse engineered for their private keys (Certik, 2024).

Another category of social engineering is 'authorised fraud', whereby victims authorise a transaction under false pretences. A key example of this is 'pig butchering' scams, in which victims are approached by what they think is a wealthy investor or romantic interest that grooms them ('fattens them up'), only to trick them into participating in a fake trading platform where they commit and lose funds (Cyvers.ai, 2025).

Other Web3-specific attacks

Many other vulnerabilities plague blockchain security. For example, a critical vulnerability in private key management resulted in the $30 million loss at the time of the Parity Multisig wallet hack in 2017 (OpenZeppelin, 2017). The rise of Non-Fungible Tokens (NFTs) and Web3 applications (DApps) introduces other security threats. One common issue is NFT wash trading and market manipulation, where traders artificially inflate the value of NFTs by buying and selling them between controlled wallets. Another growing concern is malicious airdrops and drainer attacks, where attackers distribute free NFTs or tokens that, when interacted with, exploit wallet permissions and drain funds. Front-end exploits have also become more frequent, where hackers compromise Web3 interfaces to redirect transactions to malicious smart contracts. This was seen in the BadgerDAO hack of 2021 in which BadgerDAO was impacted by an exploit of an entirely different organisation's front-end (an application called Safe), resulting in a loss of approximately $120 million (Be'ery, 2021). This has also been seen in relation to hardware wallet signing events (see Chapter 6). Furthermore, there are other classes of economic attacks, such as 'pump-and-dump' schemes where token prices are deliberately manipulated to inflate and then sell at a profit, thus 'dumping' the token value.

The industry approach to blockchain security

Addressing the blockchain security threat landscape necessitates a multifaceted approach that integrates technical, economic and social strategies. On the technical front, practices such as code audits and 'formal verification' (where mathematical methods are used to rigorously prove the correctness of smart contracts) are employed to identify vulnerabilities prior to deployment. Mechanisms such as multisignature wallets, hardware wallets and two-factor authentication offer additional layers of protection for private keys, reducing the risk of unauthorised access or theft. Meanwhile, decentralised oracles and anti-MEV solutions are deployed to counteract data manipulation and extraction strategies that can undermine transactional integrity.[9] Furthermore, network-level defences, including continuous monitoring and anomaly detection systems, aim to identify and mitigate Sybil attacks, DDoS and other adversarial attacks at scale.[10]

However, despite the growing sophistication of these tools and practices, the current approach to blockchain security remains incomplete at protecting protocols and users. Technical safeguards often function as a single point-in-time check in siloed domains. Furthermore, security services or automated tools from external audit firms can be prohibitively expensive for open-source startup projects, meaning that DeFi protocols often launch without them.

As such, these measures fail to address the systemic and sociotechnical nature of vulnerabilities that span protocol design, user behaviour and interdependencies between decentralised applications.

While social and legal initiatives such as community education initiatives and regulatory oversight contribute to building security awareness and mitigating social engineering risks, these efforts are frequently fragmented, reactive or fail to understand the ideological tenets of a decentralised industry. For example, regulators often push for the centralisation and oversight of data (via centralised Know Your Customer [KYC] and Anti-Money Laundering [AML] databases), which is antithetical to blockchain values of decentralisation and privacy. As blockchain ecosystems grow in terms of complexity and interdependencies, security must be understood not as a set of discrete solutions but as an ongoing process of governance, coordination and collective responsibility across diverse stakeholders – pervaded by insecurity.

The (fractured) blockchain security industry

The blockchain security industry, despite its importance in responding to threats, remains highly fragmented, with a diverse range of players operating under competing incentives. This fragmentation is evident in the way security efforts are distributed across different aspects of blockchain ecosystems.

Blockchain security stakeholders include protocol developers, security firms (both audit service providers and automation tooling providers), internal security teams (for projects, protocols, foundations and/or DAOs), bug bounty platforms (traditional and 'competitive'), bounty hunters, white hat hackers and policymakers. Other actors include insurance providers and users. While a significant amount of attention is directed towards technical software code audits, other equally critical areas, such as operational security for protection against social engineering attacks, often receive far less emphasis. As a result, security solutions tend to be reactive rather than proactive, addressing only specific technical risks while leaving broader systemic vulnerabilities unaddressed.

A primary focal point of the blockchain security industry is smart contract auditing. Given the high financial stakes involved in DeFi and blockchain-based applications, firms specialising in security audits conduct rigorous code reviews to identify vulnerabilities before deployment. These audits, often carried out for a handsome price, help detect re-entrancy bugs, logic errors and improper access controls – all of which have been exploited in past attacks. However, the emphasis on code audits, while an important factor, can create a false sense of security. Many protocols that have been audited have still subsequently been exploited (for example, the Rekt leaderboard – an informal ranking of the biggest financial losses, often due to hacks, exploits, liquidations, scams or poor trading decisions – shows that the second and third largest hacks in history have been due to unaudited software code [Rekt News, n.d.b]). While bugs may be identified and addressed in a contract audited in isolation, exploits can arise from unexpected interactions between contracts, oracle manipulations or economic design flaws that audits alone cannot fully mitigate.

In contrast, operational security techniques and training for defence against social engineering receive far less attention, despite their increasing role in blockchain-related attacks. Many of the most devastating exploits are not due to software flaws but rather human error, credential compromise and phishing techniques. In other words, 'security goes waaay beyond on-chain and smart contracts exclusively', as stated by Mehdi Zerouali, a co-director of Sigma Prime at DeFi Security Summit in 2024 (DeFi Security Summit, 2024b: at 6:24). Attackers often bypass the cryptographic security of the blockchain by targeting individuals and organisations through SIM swapping, phishing emails, insider threats and address poisoning scams. Despite this, few security firms specialise in training teams, improving access control policies and implementing robust security frameworks to protect against these types of attacks. The lack of standardised operational security guidelines in the blockchain space leaves users and organisations highly vulnerable to social engineering tactics.

Misalignment of incentives further exacerbates these issues. Many blockchain security firms operate as for-profit entities that benefit from the high demand for quick, transactional audits rather than long-term security strategies. Security firms compete for customers and are incentivised to charge high fees for one-time audits, whereas security vulnerabilities evolve over time, requiring continuous monitoring and upgrades, often which cannot be fully outsourced. Due to the cost of security experts to conduct these audits, the barrier to audit can easily be upwards of $100,000 USD, before a project is even launched. As a result, many DeFi protocols launch without being audited, or prioritise receiving an 'audit certification' for marketing purposes to acquire users rather than conducting rigorous, ongoing security assessments. Additionally, once an audit is completed, security firms are not responsible for post-deployment vulnerabilities or unforeseen attack vectors, resulting in a lack of accountability.

For security across the blockchain ecosystem to mature, a paradigmatic shift toward ecosystem-wide security approaches that acknowledge the insecure nature of decentralised digital infrastructure is necessary. While code audits remain essential, they must be paired with operational security best practices, real-time monitoring, and adversarial threat modelling that takes software and human vulnerabilities into account. Furthermore, incentive misalignment must be addressed to encourage long-term security commitments and decentralised security collaborations rather than focusing solely on static, pre-deployment audits. Without this shift, the blockchain ecosystem will continue to experience high-profile attacks that expose its underlying security weaknesses.

Projects and users

The fractured nature of blockchain security ecosystems often leaves users exposed and disoriented, struggling to navigate a landscape where responsibility is diffuse and unevenly distributed. Even if protocol developers and security teams implement technical safeguards, these measures rarely extend to user protection in a comprehensive or coordinated way. At the same time, users are expected to manage their own operational security, interpret complex risks and discern legitimate protocols from malicious ones, often without adequate tools or knowledge.

As Josselin Feist, independent security researcher (and former blockchain engineering director at well-known security audit firm Trail of Bits), states: 'at the end of the day, you own security. If you are building a protocol, if you are building a project, security is your responsibility. If you think an external provider is going to run security for you, you are not going to make it in the long term' (Defi Security Summit, 2024b: at 6:24). In blockchain, security cannot be outsourced to any external providers.

The danger of this approach is the burden of responsibility it places on users, who have very little recourse against a project when something goes wrong. Independent crypto investigator and white hat ZachXBT is explicit about the personal responsibility of cryptocurrency users in a post shared via his announcement-only Telegram channel, 'Investigations by ZachXBT':

> If you make either of these decisions it is your own personal choice to risk funds and I will NOT help you:
>
> 1). Deposit funds in a forked DeFi protocol on a new EVM [Ethereum Virtual Machine] chain that later gets exploited (team did not write original code; low amount of technical skills required)
> 2). Get rugged by a project with very few Kaito [AI] smart followers (at least do the bare minimum due diligence to not fall victim to fake followers or meaningless buzzwords). (Investigations by ZachXBT, semi-private comm.)

Although blockchain promotes a culture of individual control and responsibility for one's digital assets, blockchain security is inherently a collective effort. Samczsun commented in the SEAL chat:

> I think long term we have to stop pretending like the majority of users actually 'dyor' [Do Your Own Research] or whatever…In other words the idea that 'we just empower users with all the information they need to make an informed choice' doesn't work in the world where most people barely have enough of an attention span to see that they clicked on a link that said 'CLAIM AIRDROP NOW OR YOU'LL LOSE GENERATIONAL WEALTH' and their wallet said

'hey are you really sure you want to approve this transaction on this sketchy website' because they just want to print.

SEAL 911 co-founder and lead white hat hacker pcaversaccio characterised the development requirements for users in crypto software development as follows:

> If you build a crypto project for the masses, these are the people you are developing it for:
>
> - I yolo sign shit when I'm drunk at 3am
> - I fell in love with a random Chinese woman on a Tinder-like app and invested my pension funds into an investment scam
> - I store my seed phrase on paper and think it's a cold storage but I took an image first of it and synced it with my Google Drive which doesn't have 2FA
> - I'm searching a job online and enjoy downloading everything that random people share with me
> - I got a recommendation of a friend and now invested all of my savings into the next-gen-100000qbits-AI-crypto-to-the-Jupyter project and realise now that there is a 100% transfer fee. (pcaversaccio, 2024a)

In response to this post on X, some people retorted the comment: 'web2 fixes this' (itsjustcornbro, 2024). Yet, from what we know about exploits against centralised services, whether data or money, this is not necessarily accurate.

The fragmentation of the blockchain security industry results in a security gap, where neither party – developer nor user – holds full responsibility, and both are vulnerable to the consequences of hacks and security failures. Failure can look like both individual losses for users, as well as industry reputational damage in the eyes of lawmakers interested in consumer protection, who become the fallback authority to provide recourse but are often slow and reactive themselves in the face of a fast-paced, ever-evolving industry landscape. In recognition of this, blockchain security is a shared obligation, requiring both robust infrastructure and secure code, as well as user education, responsive design and collaborative governance to identify insecurities and begin to address them.

Don't trust, verify

As blockchain applications grow more complex, and this complexity is not abstracted away from end users at the application level, the advised mindset from pcaversaccio is to 'BE FUCKING PARANOID ABOUT EVERYTHING YOU TOUCH IN THIS SPACE :)' (ethnographic interview).

The message arising from security breaches is that where there is a will, there is a way. If Web3 is to become a workable alternative to some of the failings of Web2, people need to unlearn the convenience of Web2 and learn to secure their own assets. Even so, there is a role for the collective security provision in the race between security experts and hackers, as users increasingly require techniques that extend beyond general consumer knowledge and abilities.

Conclusion

Despite being built on foundations of privacy, cryptography and technical systems that disintermediate trust, the current state of blockchain security is marked by precarity and persistent vulnerability. This condition stems not only from the inherent characteristics of decentralised infrastructure but also from the evolving threat landscape and often fragmented ways in which the ecosystem responds. The ideological commitments and architectural constraints of decentralised systems raise important questions about how security is conceptualised, implemented and maintained without centralised authorities and in the face of multifaceted and serious threats. These dynamics demand closer examination of how decentralised technology communities navigate the challenge of securing open systems. By exploring how decentralised actors coordinate in the face of complex, shifting risks, we can begin to understand what decentralised technology communities can teach us about the broader practice of digital security. The next chapter turns to this question of coordination, examining how blockchain security is organised among stakeholders.

Table 2.2 Blockchain security industry taxonomy

Stakeholders	
Security firms (software auditors)	Professional teams that audit smart contracts and blockchain protocols for vulnerabilities.
Bug bounty hunters	Independent individuals who find and report vulnerabilities in exchange for rewards.
Bug bounty platforms	Platforms like Immunefi or HackerOne that facilitate bounty programmes between projects and researchers.
Protocol security teams	Internal teams dedicated to ensuring the ongoing security of a specific blockchain or DApp.
Users	Everyday participants in blockchain systems who are often targeted by scams or social engineering.
Insurance providers	Offer financial protection against hacks and exploits for protocols and users.
Protocol developers	Build and maintain blockchain codebases and smart contracts, often on the front line of responding to vulnerabilities.
White hat hackers	Ethical hackers who identify and responsibly disclose vulnerabilities/ aid in blockchain protocol/fund rescues.
Grey hat hackers	Skilled hackers to may or may not choose to responsible disclose vulnerabilities or exploit them for personal gain.
Policymakers	Regulators and government actors who shape the legal frameworks surrounding blockchain technologies.
Foundations	Organisational bodies that support ecosystem development, funding and security practices.

(Continued)

Table 2.2 (Continued)

Node operators (known as 'miners' in Proof of Work or 'validators' in Proof of Stake)	Maintain blockchain networks; their behaviour affects network integrity and security.
Wallet providers	Custodial and non-custodial services offering user-facing tools to store private keys securely.
Exchanges (centralised [CEX] and decentralised [DEX])	Platforms for token trading, often targeted by high-profile attacks.
Cybersecurity researchers/academics	Analyse blockchain vulnerabilities and contribute theoretical insights and tools.
Incident response and analytics firms	Help trace stolen funds and analyse post-hack incidents.
MEV searchers/builders	Actors exploiting or optimising Miner/MEV strategies, sometimes straddling ethical lines.
Black hat hackers/Adversaries (see breakdown below under 'Threat Actors'	Malicious actors who exploit vulnerabilities or engage in criminal activities.

Threat Actors

Crypto natives	Technologically sophisticated insiders exploiting complex systems for personal gain.
Criminal APTs	Organised groups often with financial or geopolitical motives.
Nation-state APTs	State-sponsored actors targeting infrastructure or assets for intelligence or disruption.
Malicious insiders	Individuals within organisations who intentionally compromise security.
Amateur attackers	Inexperienced hackers using pre-written tools for opportunistic attacks (for example, 'script kiddies').
Automated bots/botnets	Scripts or networks used for spam, front-running or brute-force attacks.

(Continued)

Table 2.2 (Continued)

Attacks	
Protocol-level attacks	Attacks on consensus or core protocol design flaws.
Cryptographic weaknesses	Exploiting flawed cryptographic implementations or primitives.
Smart contract exploits	Bugs or logic flaws that enable unauthorised actions.
Network and infrastructure attacks	Includes DDoS, Sybil attacks and attacks on hosting infrastructure.
Economic attacks	Exploiting incentive misalignments or arbitrage opportunities in protocol design.
Flash loan exploits	Using instant, uncollateralised loans to manipulate protocol behaviour.
Liquidity pool manipulation	Draining or manipulating prices within automated market makers (AMMs).
Replay attacks (on forks or Layers 2s (L2s))	Reusing valid transactions from one chain on another to exploit discrepancies.

Scams	
Social engineering	Deceiving users into revealing sensitive information (e.g. phishing, impersonation).
Operational security failures	Poor key management or exposed credentials leading to compromise.
Rug pulls	Developers intentionally withdraw liquidity or disappear after token sales.
Phishing (on-chain and off-chain)	Fake sites, links or contracts used to steal assets.
Impersonation/fake social media accounts	Mimicking official channels to deceive users.
Pump-and-dump/token manipulation	Artificially inflating token prices before mass selling for profit at the expense of other token holders when the token value deflates.

Table 2.3 Cryptocurrency hack/attack trend timeline

2014: Exchange compromise

- Mt. Gox Exchange Hack: once handling 70 per cent of all Bitcoin transactions, Mt. Gox suffered a catastrophic breach resulting in the loss of approximately 850,000 BTC (worth around $450 million at the time). The attack exploited security flaws in the exchange's infrastructure, leading to its bankruptcy.

2016: Smart contract exploits

- The DAO Attack: a DAO built on Ethereum was exploited due to a vulnerability in its smart contract code which allowed the attacker to 'call' the same withdrawal function numerous times. The attacker siphoned about 3.6 million ETH (valued at roughly $50 million), prompting a controversial hard fork in the Ethereum blockchain to reverse the damage.

2017: Code vulnerabilities

- Parity Multisig Wallet Hack: a flaw in the Parity Ethereum client allowed an attacker to exploit a bug in the multisignature wallet code, resulting in the theft of approximately 153,000 ETH (worth around $30 million at the time).

2018: Exchange compromise

- Coincheck Hack: Japanese exchange Coincheck was compromised, leading to the loss of about $530 million worth of NEM tokens. The breach was attributed to inadequate security measures, including the lack of multisignature wallet protocols and storing assets in hot (internet connected) wallets, rather than cold storage (offline).

2021: Cross-chain bridge exploits

- Poly Network Exploit: attackers exploited vulnerabilities in Poly Network's cross-chain bridge contracts, transferring over $610 million in various cryptocurrencies to their own addresses. Remarkably, the hacker returned the majority of the funds, citing ethical motivations.

2022: Validator node compromise

- Ronin Network Hack: the Ronin Network, an Ethereum sidechain used for the game Axie Infinity, suffered a breach where attackers used hacked private keys to withdraw $625 million in ETH and USDC. The exploit involved compromising five of the nine validator nodes, highlighting the importance of decentralised validator structures.

(Continued)

Table 2.3 (Continued)

2023: Flash loan attacks

- Various DeFi Protocols: flash loans – unsecured loans that must be borrowed and repaid within a single transaction – were used to manipulate DeFi protocols, leading to significant losses. Attackers exploited price oracle manipulations and re-entrancy bugs, emphasising the need for robust smart contract design and accurate price feeds.

2024: Front-end compromises and social engineering

- Velodrome Front-End Attack: hackers compromised the front-end interface of the Velodrome protocol, leading to over $100,000 in losses. This incident demonstrated that even if smart contracts are secure, vulnerabilities in user interfaces can be exploited to deceive users.
- Address-Poisoning Attacks: using techniques like CREATE2, attackers pre-generated large numbers of potential addresses to conduct address-poisoning attacks, tricking users into sending funds to malicious addresses that closely resemble legitimate ones.

2025: Supply chain attacks

- Safe (multisignature wallet) Compromise: North Korean hackers infiltrated the Safe infrastructure by compromising a developer's machine, injecting malicious JavaScript into the wallet's website. This targeted Bybit's signers, leading to the theft of $1.5 billion (see Chapter 6).
- Phemex Exchange Breach: an attacker drained $73.54 million from Phemex's hot wallets across nearly thirty different blockchain networks. The breach underscored the risks associated with managing multiple hot wallets and the importance of stringent access controls.

Ongoing: Social engineering and human exploits

- Discord admin takeovers, address poisoning, fake airdrops: exploiting people and social channels instead of code.
- Lazarus Group phishing: spear phishing to access validator or developer credentials.

Note: regarding the ten largest cryptocurrency hacks by USD value at the time of the incident, each incident includes the failure-mode (i.e. what was compromised), the coordination-pattern (i.e. how stakeholders tried to contain it), the threat actor (i.e. who perpetrated the attack) and whether or not funds were returned (if known).

Table 2.4 Blockchain security actor incentive landscape

Security stakeholder	Typology of stance	Incentive/Legitimacy claim
White hat (civic-rescuer)	Prioritises harm reduction and restitution for users. Morally bound and fee-averse.	Duty of care, visible harm prevention, community mandate.
White hat (protocol-guardian)	Aligned with a project/DAO. Emphasises continuity of core infrastructure.	Stewardship of shared infrastructure/ governance mandate.
Bounty hunter (skilled pragmatist)	Competes for posted rewards from protocols or bounty platforms. Optimises for payout efficiency and contractual framing.	Contractual compliance, 'plays by the rules'.
Security firm (mercenary-responder)	Third-party specialists/firms emphasising capability, speed, professionalism and reputation. Typically operate on premium fees. May have served previously as security advisors or auditors for a protocol. Frequently operate in war rooms alongside white hats.	Capability and outcomes; risk assumed.
Independent researcher (blockchain sleuth)	Often pseudonymous; driven by investigative interest and altruism, though may accept compensation. Contributes to industry alerting and collective defence.	Ecosystem stewardship, knowledge mandate.
Grey hat hacker	Enacts rescue theatre for personal gain: exploits protocols while insisting on white hat framing (e.g. choosing to exploit a vulnerability instead of engaging in responsible disclosure; ransom-style return conditions; insists on white hat narrative framing).	Legitimacy claimed via protocol rules and self-framed narratives.
Black hat hacker	Unapologetically exploits protocols and users.	Pure financial gain. No legitimacy claim.

Table 2.5 Cryptocurrency hack timeline

Number	Value	Date	Name	Failure mode	Coordination pattern	Threat actor	Funds returned
1.	$1.5 billion	2025	Bybit (exchange)	Compromised Safe Wallet interface to target a cold-to-hot-wallet transfer process.	CEO announcements on social media channels, industry blocklists, independent security researcher funds tracing, white hat requests to freeze protocols (i.e. mixers where funds being laundered).	Democratic People's Republic of Korea (DPRK) 'TraderTraitor' (Lazarus subgroup).	No, but user losses reimbursed by Bybit.
2.	$624 million	2022	Ronin/Axie Infinity (bridge/validators)	Validator key compromise (5-of-9).	War room, partner escalation to contain cascade effect.	DPRK (Lazarus Group).	Partially (approximately $30 million seized; additional small tranches later). Users reimbursed via investor financing.
3.	$611 million	2021	Poly Network (cross-chain protocol)	Authorisation logic flaw.	White hat war room, public negotiation; white hat return narrative; stablecoin issuer freeze.	Self-named 'Mr White Hat' hacker or hackers.	Yes (nearly all returned within about fifteen days).
4.	$586 million	2022	BNB Chain ('Token Hub')	Proof–verification weakness allowing forged messages.	Security researcher and white hat, chain halt and patch, partner freezing, on-chain governance updates.	Unknown.	Majority frozen on BNB Chain. Approximately $137 million moved off-chain and not returned. Losses covered by Binance.

5.	$530 million	2018	Coincheck (exchange)	Private key compromise of currency stored in hot wallet not cold wallet with no multisignature procedure.	Delayed internal alerts. Exchange withdrawals frozen. Federal investigations.	DPRK Lazarus.	No. Exchange promised 90 per cent repayment.
6.	$477 million	2022	FTX (exchange)	SIM-swap and social-engineering amid FTX exchange bankruptcy chaos and Sam Bankman-Fried court proceedings.	FBI investigation.	Three Americans tied to criminal group 'Powell SIM Swapping Crew'.	No.
7.		2014	Mt. Gox (exchange)	Long-running hot-wallet theft discovered at bankruptcy.	Federal investigation.	The US Justice Department has charged two Russian nationals – Alexey Bilyuchenko and Aleksandr Verner – with hacking Mt. Gox and laundering roughly 647,000 BTC taken from the exchange, valued at around $400 million USD at the time.	No.

(Continued)

Table 2.5 (Continued)

Number	Value	Date	Name	Failure mode	Coordination pattern	Threat actor	Funds returned
8.	$326 million	2022	Wormhole (Solana bridge)	Signature/ verification bug enabling unauthorised mint.	White hat alert, war room, patch and post-mortem.	Unknown.	No, despite a $10 million bounty offered. Users and the protocol were backstopped by 'Jump Crypto' developer/trader team.
9.	$304 million	2024	DMM Bitcoin (exchange)	Social-engineering and malware attack enabling manipulation of the wallet transfer process via session-cookie exploit.	Reported by 'Whale Alert' (live reporting on large blockchain transactions). FBI, Department of Defense Cyber Crime Center and National Police Agency of Japan issued public alerts and investigations.	DPRK 'TraderTraitor' (Lazarus subgroup).	No. Users reimbursed via capital raise/ transfer.
10.	$280 million	2020	KuCoin (exchange)	Hot-wallet key compromise.	Internal risk-management system flagged abnormal transactions and hot-wallet balances. The exchange then moved remaining funds to cold storage and began partner escalation (including issuer freezes (i.e. Tether stablecoin), token re-issues (i.e. Orion, Velo, NOIA), exchanges blocking addresses, on-chain tracking and law enforcement investigation.	DPRK Lazarus.	84 per cent of funds recovered. KuCoin covered the remainder via its insurance fund.

Notes

1 A cryptocurrency hardware wallet is a physical device that stores the private keys needed to access and manage your cryptocurrencies offline, with the intention of providing an additional layer of security against attacks.
2 All SEAL chat quotes and mentions refer to personal, private communications. Some communications have intentionally been anonymised.
3 All SEAL chat quotes and mentions refer to personal, private communications. Some communications have intentionally been anonymised.
4 A bridge is a mechanism that enables interoperability between different blockchain platforms to allow assets or data to move between two separate blockchain networks. Bridges are often high-value targets and have been the site of some of the largest exploits in Web3, often due to design flaws or compromised validators.
5 An automated piece of software (script or programme) runs from a central system to perform malicious activities at speed and/or scale, for example, executing a large number of transactions to spam a network or extracting value through techniques like frontrunning.
6 According to Security Researcher Craig (x86NOP), the 51% Attack concern was primarily a concern in the early days of blockchain networks, when their scale was still small. Blockchains are designed to be decentralised so that no single entity can control the system or its outcomes. The concern was that if the network consisted of only a limited number of nodes while the value of the token increased, an attacker might find it economically feasible to gain 51 per cent of the network's validation power. Controlling a majority of the validation is effectively equivalent to hijacking the chain: the attacker could determine which transactions are included in blocks. In a simple illustrative scenario, they could insert a series of transactions that redirect funds from high-value wallets to one under their own control. In the early days, this risk was mitigated by miners distributing their participation across different mining pools to ensure no single pool approached a majority stake. The transition from Proof of Work (PoW) to Proof of Stake (PoS) further reduced this risk, and a 51 per cent attack is widely considered a solved problem in contemporary large-scale blockchain networks.
7 A 'memetic' piece of media – such as an image, phrase or video – that spreads rapidly online, often with humorous or symbolic meaning. In crypto, a 'meme' can also refer to meme coins or tokens that gain value and popularity primarily through social media hype rather than fundamental utility.

8 A grifter is a person who engages in deception or manipulation to swindle others, often for personal financial gain. In the crypto space, grifters typically promote scams, pump-and-dump schemes or misleading projects while concealing their true intentions.

9 Miner/MEV: the total value a block producer can extract from transaction manipulation in the block they produce, beyond the standard block reward and gas fees, by strategically ordering or censoring transactions.

10 Distributed Denial-of-Service attack: a cyberattack in which the perpetrator seeks to make a machine or network resource unavailable to its intended users by temporarily or indefinitely disrupting the services of a host connected to a network.

Part II

How decentralised security is organised

3

Blockchain white hat hackers

Introduction

The previous chapters have traced the historical, ideological and contextual foundations of blockchain security, from the early visions of hackers, cryptographers and Cypherpunks to the emergence of decentralised protocols and the burgeoning security landscape. This chapter introduces a new protagonist in the security landscape: the blockchain white hat hacker. Far from operating in the shadows, these actors play a vital role in the moral, political and economic landscape of blockchains by helping to safeguard decentralised systems. This chapter examines the practices, motivations and incentives – financial, moral, and reputational – that drive white hat activity, highlighting how these individuals contribute to vulnerability disclosure, incident response and the overall resilience of the blockchain ecosystem. In doing so, it situates white hats as key stakeholders in the decentralised security landscape.

'What to do when your device is completely compromised'

A painful message appeared in the '#general' channel of the communication platform Slack for an organisation I'm in:

Dearest Colleagues,
Some bad news to report and a warning – 'John' and I got phished/hacked, crypto wallets drained from a link/downloaded file from a business development Lead to a cryptocurrency related Research Group...

A 'VCs granting org' called 'Pixels VC' had reached out interested in research group and we talked to the guy since December in the Telegram chat application trying to line up a call. He sent a meeting link for us to join what we thought was a video call yesterday morning and a file was downloaded, then he deleted the chat and disappeared. I had a weird feeling and checked my crypto wallets and there was a drainer contract. Joe's wallets were also drained. We both lost significant amounts of savings from work over the last several years.

We have no idea what was in the file, or what it does/is doing to our computers so we shut them down and are looking for help do a factory reset/wipe and scan. Please let us know if you all have technical experience or contacts for any cybersecurity people that can advise best practices in the case the file doesn't scan as a virus, still have the file too if anyone has a quarantine analysis set up.

We contacted SEAL 911 [Security Alliance 911 team] and known white hat groups and are pursuing help there, not much they can do for what is gone, but there is still some crypto on time lock that we tried to retrieve.

White hats sent this doc for security checklist and best practices fyi:https://docs.google.com/document/d/1HF3CJmxvWQNydaECgj huXluVtiIN1t4Sl4CUJn4Bqr4/edit?tab=t.0 [The document is entitled 'What to do when your device is completely compromised', and begins with 'Hello! We have reason to believe your computer is compromised. Your assets & accounts are at risk'. For a persistent link to SEAL resources, see: https://securityalliance.org/go/malware].

We went through the word doc checklist, changed passwords, secured 2fa on emails, password accounts, Twitter, Telegram, signed out of all instances across devices and shut off our computers – contacted workplace operations team who are taking appropriate action to change company passwords just in case. The white hats say they are mostly after crypto/Twitter/Telegram accounts access but we don't know for sure. Don't want to alarm you but just be aware, and report or ask if you see anything fishy.

And a warning – I have been in crypto for over a decade and this is my 2nd phishing attack I've endured. Don't store too much crypto on hot wallets like metamask, and do always trust your intuition and try and slow down to think through when clearing transactions or downloading anything.

We are pretty devastated so also may be slower to respond and work as we are working from mobile until laptops can get wiped.

Thank you for your attention and support and be safe.[1]

Hacker culture

Hackers are individuals or organisations that are skilled in software systems and use their abilities to gain unauthorised access to computer systems, networks or devices. The origins of the term 'hacker' trace back to the early use of computers in the 1960s, when the word referred to highly skilled and enthusiastic computer programmers who enjoyed exploring and testing the technical capabilities of a computing system. Developer and advocate of open source software, Eric Raymond, refers to hackers in this early period as a group of 'particularly creative people who define themselves partly by rejection of "normal" values and working habits', with shared experiences, folk tales, jokes and values but brimming with subcultures (Raymond, 1991: 1). Gabriella Coleman, an anthropologist known for documenting and commenting on the activities of the international hacker group Anonymous, also frames the heterogeneous nature of hacker morality not as a concrete set of doctrines but a cultural sensibility that is continually being negotiated and reformed amidst points of tension (Coleman and Golub, 2008).

The politics and practices of hacking are both a social and cultural phenomenon, with sweeping implications for individual and geopolitical security. This phenomenon and its consequences are amplified by digitisation. Early portrayals of hackers paint them as computing heroes who utilise the power of cryptography to rebel against big government in pursuit of privacy in an emerging digital era of surveillance. Hackers are typically committed to principles of intellectual freedom, free speech, transparency and meritocracy, which are expressed in their 'tinkering' with software and hardware (Coleman, 2012: 3). These principles are embodied in their belief that software should be open source for people to use, modify and distribute, and that this should be legally reflected in software licensing. The ethic of early hackers is epitomised in the phrases: 'information should be free', and 'mistrust authority – promote decentralization' [of information systems and power structures] (Levy, 1984: 26–36; 1999). This representation of hackers has been appropriated by legislators and the media, who interpret hacker practices as an antagonistic threat to the interests of established corporate and government powers (as the forces behind intellectual property and order) (Nissenbaum, 2004). The tension between skilled software makers/breakers and government authorities can be observed in heavy-handed State responses to high-profile cases of hacking, such as those of Edward Snowdon and Julian Assange (Munro and Kenny, 2023).

Over time, the term 'hacker' became associated with both legitimate and illegitimate activities. White hat hackers pursue higher-order moral hacking activities. They use their skills in accordance with and pursuit of certain ethics, for example, improving software by finding and reporting security vulnerabilities, or intervening in a compromised protocol to support victim/s during a crisis. White hat hackers may be found working for security companies or operating independently to win competitive software flaw discovery rewards, known as 'bug bounties'. On the other hand, black hat hackers exploit systems for malicious purposes and personal benefit, such as stealing data or funds. Then somewhere oscillating between the two, perhaps even depending on interests and incentives, are the grey hat hackers, who may violate ethical norms or laws in pursuit of a higher purpose goal, such as exposing vulnerabilities to the public to achieve their interpretation of the common good (Coleman, 2012). For example, when musing about how a bug bounty platform could be hacked to gain access to and profit from sensitive intelligence, the lead of SEAL 911 pcaversaccio said, 'yes there are two wolves inside me lol' to the SEALs, referring to the white hat hacker that is motivated by ideology and altruism, and the grey hat hacker that is motivated by incentives, technical prowess and reputation (private communication, SEAL chat).

In an interview with Isaac Patka, founder of Shield3 security firm and leader of SEAL's attack simulation (Wargames) team, he points out that in the early days of smart contract enabled public blockchains, there was little distinction between white hats and black hats (as those willing to exploit computational systems for personal gain at the expense of others). Many projects released protocols without investing in costly professional security audits. Instead, they relied on hackers to identify and exploit vulnerabilities, often preemptively offering bug bounties as a reward, or offering them after disclosure. Patka reflected that the approach as a security expert at this time was more or less, 'Let's all try to wreck protocols as much as possible and see what survives' (ethnographic interview). He explained how he had never been very concerned about formal agreements and remuneration, instead trusting and experiencing that he was usually paid in retrospect for valuable hacking efforts. It is from comments such as these that we start to see the continuities from bygone hacker cultures as well as the unique characteristics of a particular breed of hackers: blockchain hackers.

Blockchain white hat hackers

While the immutable nature of blockchain protocols is founded on built-in cryptographic guarantees and automation, hacking hinges on the combination of protocols and people. White hat hackers have played a crucial role in the history and development of the cryptocurrency industry. They are responsible for rescuing millions of dollars of cryptocurrency funds each year (Cavez-Dreyfuss and Wilson, 2021). A well-known example of white hat response is the infamous hack of 'The DAO' in 2016 (DuPont, 2017), in which white hats exploited the re-entry bug in the smart contract as it was being exploited in real time to draw out funds in real time and rescue them from the black hat hacker. Yet, little data exists on how white hat hackers, as key actors in blockchain networks, fit into the landscape of blockchain security.

The white hat label is a claim to legitimacy, rather than an intrinsic status. Following Coleman's insight that hacker worlds mesh craft with ethics, blockchain white hats narrate their interventions along four justificatory strands: (1) civic rescue ('users first') and protocol stewardship (defending the commons, such as professional and independent security expert volunteers seeking to recover funds from compromised protocols, returning them safely and crafting post-mortem communications to prevent future exploits); (2) craft honour (competence, speed, elegance – arguably a necessary trait for any hacker to successfully rescue or hack funds and earn reputation); (3) protocol stewardship (defending the commons); and (4) market pragmatism (bounties, fees and rewards, such as organisational security professionals, bug bounty hunters and independent security experts helping to secure smart contracts and improve vulnerabilities – as well as exploiters seeking to identify and exploit vulnerabilities without permission [sometimes paying back stolen funds for a reward, and sometimes not]). These strands overlap among individuals and incidents, often with ideology taking precedence in the narrative of events, while the practicality of financial incentives for sustainability remains a driving motive.

These justificatory stances are also tested under pressure – such as when rescues are conducted like ransoms, when disclosure practices are contested, or when infiltrators mimic white hat scripts but act with sketchy motives, such as hacking funds rather than responsible disclosure. White hats also have to safeguard their own security. If a rescue fails, a project deems their actions malicious, or their moral drivers don't align with those of the government, they face ongoing legal risk and repercussions.

In practice, white hats present themselves less as a fixed moral category and more as a stance that is played out repeatedly over time to prove competence and reputation. The role is distinguished from adjacent security stakeholder roles (i.e. salaried security professionals that work for a private firm, bug bounty hunters or independent researchers) through justificatory narratives and boundary work. Their self-positioning leans on personal narratives of civic rescue (protecting users) and commons stewardship (defending protocols), which they contrast with the commercial obligations of corporate responders and the pragmatism and margin for error of bounty hunting. Blockchain white hats position themselves as the heroes of blockchain security, fighting tirelessly for the good of the industry and for little reward.

As well as self-designation of the white hat label, group boundaries are maintained through rituals and gates. These rituals include volunteer contributions to blockchain security efforts, demonstrated competence in rescues, vouching for others' reputations to enter private channels, vocalising dismay at hacks/poor security practices and repeated constructive contributions to both private (i.e. war rooms) and to open-source (i.e. incident post-mortems, intelligence sharing or software) security artefacts. The epitome of blockchain white hat hacker-hood was being invited to participate on a voluntary basis in live war rooms, which demanded extreme technical prowess, confidentiality, stakeholder coordination and 24/7 dedication to checking and responding in chat channels for no immediate personal financial gain. These boundaries and practices enabled coordination on who is entitled to intervene, on what terms and with whose consent. These are combined with the necessary infrastructure to coordinate a priori consent for white hats to intervene in blockchain protocol exploits, as explored in Chapter 4 (i.e. the Safe Harbor initiative).

SEAL's practical labour (or boundary work) as a new organisation (although led by well-known white hat reputations) in drawing, defending, and revising the lines that separate legitimate from illegitimate actors and actions makes the blockchain white hat category usable. The numerous initiatives founded by the organisation, explored in detail in Chapter 4, form boundary objects: the artefacts that carry this work across otherwise disjointed ecosystems to coordinate action without requiring consensus on values and identity. Security practitioners enforce each other's 'good faith' behaviours through sharing of conduct (for example, who reported first, whether users were harmed and rewards), and via reputation practice (i.e. vouching, membership, channel access and the ability to influence discussions and governance decisions). They also expel negative behaviour via public callouts (both in private chats or public posts on X), blacklist bad actors (by creating block lists of nefarious wallet addresses) and downgrade reputations by removing people from security group chats and war rooms. The white hat category's permeability is both a strength – allowing rapid, federated response as well as coordination, mentorship and celebration of desired contributions – and a liability – relying on responsible boundary making by reputable leaders, as well as creating the risk of rogue agents masquerading as constructive contributors (although this has not occurred in SEAL to the best of my knowledge – despite fears that it could).

A SEAL chat on the topic of (the lack of) white hat statistics provides a window into the discourse surrounding how white, black and grey hats are differentiated, and why this can be problematic:[2]

Matta, co-founder of crypto security and education team the Red Guild and lead of the SEAL frameworks initiative, said: 'do we have some metrics on how many projects that were exploited a return of funds occurred? Or how many black hat attacks compared to white hats?'

Taylor Monahan ('Tayvano'), Security, Metamask and Incident Response, SEAL 911: 'Yeah the defi rekt database tracks some returns/recoveries but I wouldn't say anyone has comprehensive stats tbh'.

Matta: 'Maybe 911 experience on this would really useful. I _ feel_, and by feel i literally talk about a sensation or a personal perspective, that almost no white hat hacks really occur, or are scarce, and most of the hacks that occur don't usually end up in a return of funds. Am I wrong?

some of them are greyish, like they turn whitehat given a few conditions, or because don't see another alternative have been pressured to do it'.

Taylor: 'You are not wrong The cases where funds are returned are vast minority The cases where was ACTUAL whitehat are VERY rare…

My gut says that, count wise, there are likely the most amt of frontruns. Which are good people, good actors. But is not really the same as whitehat? But we all call them whitehat and is okay…

Then blackhats who return the funds for mix of reasons. They are still blackhats but I will call them whitehats if it inspires them to return the money. I do not call them anything after they return the money, except blackhats, in private

Then actual whitehat missions. Where people knowingly are whitehatting something. Usually bc is very risky and almost always better ways to operate these days (pause etc)'.

Matta: 'if we dig deeper the terms tend to confuse so I agree, i have never liked labeling nor "ethical hacking" terminology, hacking is ethical otherwise you're a criminal (though curiosity and hacktivisim are a separate topic and legal stuff doesn't always go well with them). I kinda hate that the term white hat has been merely used for someone who returned funds ignoring completely their initial intentions

do you know if prosecution has been made for these types of folks?'

Taylor: 'Yeah I agree. I sorta grit my teeth and do it bc, once you're in that position, calling someone a name to get the money back is always worth it. But it's not something I think we should aspire for or idolize. It's a least shitty choice out of a v limited number of shitty choices'. (SEAL Discord Chat. August 25, 2024).

In terms of prosecution, some hackers have ended up in prison for grey hat activity. For example, former senior security engineer Shakeeb Ahmed received a three-year prison sentence after hacking two decentralised cryptocurrency exchanges (US Attorney's Office, Southern District of New York, 2024). In their statement on the case, the United States Attorney's Office said 'Shakeeb Ahmed pled guilty and agreed to return all of the stolen crypto to his victims. That arrest is now the first ever conviction for such a hack' (US Attorney's Office, Southern District of New York, 2023). The Attorney's Office continued,

> Ahmed used his technical know-how to steal over $12 million and tried to cover his tracks by swapping stolen crypto for Monero, using cryptocurrency mixers, hopping across blockchains, and utilising overseas crypto exchanges. Today's conviction shows that no matter how sophisticated the methods used, fraud is fraud, and we will swiftly catch and convict you. (US Attorney's Office, Southern District of New York, 2023).

In other cases, the grey hat hackers are able to negotiate handsome bounties with the protocols in exchange for returning the funds.

In one such case where a hacker negotiated a white hat bounty, ZachXBT reports: 'A smart decision here by the hacker to negotiate a bounty & return funds (18.5% of $8.8m)'. He proceeds to comment: 'Interestingly enough they did a relatively poor job of covering their tracks' (ZachXBT, 2022), pointing out that this was not good faith, white hat behaviour but evidence of a bad and not entirely competent actor seizing an opportunity for personal financial gain.

The term 'hack backs' refers to a situation where ethical hackers exploit a vulnerability themselves, either pre-emptively or reactively, in order to protect or recover funds that would otherwise be stolen or misused by malicious actors. In some cases, it can be that white hats are able to hack black hats to beat them to an exploit and rescue funds. However, this can be controversial, as it often challenges legal and ethical lines, and hackers can be motivated by a mix of good intentions and financial incentives.

In one example, Rekt reports: '@PunkProtocol was hacked for $8.95M. ~$5M was returned by an anonymous anti-hero, but not before paying themselves $1M. White hats set their own wages, while security auditors take their salaries and the blame' (Rekt News, 2021). In this case, a white hat was able to front-run transactions amidst a hack and return over half of the funds, keeping the rest as their bounty in reward for their skill (Rekt, 2021).

Due to the public nature of blockchain, messages can be sent on-chain to communicate between hackers and projects. For example, a hacker responsible for draining $47 million from decentralised exchange protocol KyberSwap sent an on-chain message with strange demands to take control of the company by buying out executives at a fair price and doubling the salaries of employees that choose to stay – seemingly with the goal to improve the value of the token price and project (Hunt, 2023).[3] The hacker was allegedly a Canadian developer and maths aficionado who has since been indicted by the US Department of Justice (Wood, 2025). These instances demonstrate the ever-evolving, high-stakes games of cat and mouse between attackers and defenders. These interactions test both hackers and protocol security teams, and are predicated on technical prowess, confidence and courage.

In other cases, white hats really do save the day as protocol heroes. For example, security firm BlockSec prevented a hacker from stealing $5 million from the NFT lending project Paraspace. Detecting in real time that a hacker was unable to execute the attack due to low 'gas' (transaction) fees, BlockSec carried out an attack as a white hat to take control of the assets, and notified Paraspace of the events (Chawla, 2023). In a demonstration of the competitive, skill-based nature of hacking, the hacker left an on-chain message asking for their 'gas' fees to be refunded by BlockSec: 'I couldn't make it work because of a stupid gas estimation error. Since I lost a lot of money trying to make it work, it would be cool to get at least some of them back…best of luck'.

Motivations

While motivated by reputation and money, white hats are ultimately bound to ideological goals and values. They continually reinforce this publicly as part of reputation building and awareness raising practices. As stated by pcaversaccio in the SEAL chat when they shared an open-source script that they had developed: 'My personal aim…to have the majority of people actually building from day one with Cypherpunk principles and thus the protocols become ungovernable in the sense that nobody can control/censor it'. pcaversaccio continued on X:

I've seen countless folks scrambling to recover tokens from compromised wallets besieged by sweeper bots. So, I decided to take action and create an open-source (white hat) frontrunning script designed to outsmart these fuckers and recover vulnerable funds…

My hope is that this script becomes a powerful ally for victims and their tech-savvy allies, helping them reclaim at-risk funds and regain control over their assets – totally independent of any third-party support! [signed off with a salute emoji] (pcaversaccio, 2025b)

The 'Ethereum Cypherpunk Manifesto', penned and immortalised on-chain by a handful of Ethereum proponents, references the 'spirit' of the original Cypherpunk Manifesto by Eric Hughes. It outlines the core principles of privacy as a cornerstone of individual freedom; security in the design and implementation of decentralised systems; and censorship resistance in terms of thwarting all forms of censorship and gatekeeping (pcaversaccio, 2024). Based on these cultural foundations, contributors to SEAL have engaged in industry-transforming white hat rescues and ecosystem-wide coordination to improve the state of blockchain security.

This is complemented by the SEAL 911 Code of Conduct, which concisely outlines the blockchain white hat rules of engagement:

1. We Are Accountable
2. We Act Ethically
3. We Protect Our Information and Assets (Security Alliance/ SEAL 911, n.d.a)

To act ethically in this context means that white hats do not exploit information for personal gain. As briefly elaborated on in the SEAL 911 Code of Conduct, acting ethically means: 'Do not exploit any sensitive information advantage in any way to gain a personal, commercial, or other malicious advantage…**Simply put: Don't be a dick!**' (Security Alliance/SEAL 911, n.d.a).

Adhering to this code of conduct is incredibly important to white hats' reputation and integrity, as it is the only shared principle they have to operate by in distributed, pseudonymous digital domains. In other conversations in the SEAL chat, contributors exclaimed their dismay and disgust with unethical and incompetent behaviour, with one stating, 'It makes me so angry that people are not careful with others funds [sic], its substantial for some of them and you should do your god damn best to make sure they dont lose it from you being dumb'.

Of course, while principles and results are important, money still helps and is a necessary resource to sustain white hat efforts.

Incentives

The SEAL 911 emergency response team is responsible for over $100 million in rescued funds. They have been involved in war rooms (physical or virtual coordination spaces where stakeholders gather to coordinate rapid responses to a security incident) to respond to dozens of publicly disclosed rescue and support incidents, spanning white hat rescues, fake app take downs and reversing social media and web Domain Name Service (DNS) account take overs (Security Alliance/SEAL 911, n.d.b).

pcaversaccio shares in a SEAL chat: 'One recent true white hat hack example we handled in SEAL 911 was that one', linking to a screenshot of an on-chain message to hackers in a $4.8 million incident that stated: 'Hi team, this is a whitehat rescue hack. Let's work on reimbursing the users' (pcaversaccio, 2024f), with replies on X including the message: 'King', 'What a King' and using the salute emoji.

pcaversaccio goes on to explain the inner workings of the incident in the SEAL chat: 'The project hasn't replied to us and the reporter did decide to drain it. We afterwards created a group with them and returned the funds minus a 5% bounty'.

The volunteer team members that monitor the 911 emergency reporting line take their role seriously. Sharing insight into the eve ryday life of a SEAL 911 member, pcaversaccio posted on X: 'I woke up bc I had to pee and now im in a warroom' (pcaversaccio, 2024g).

Despite such dedicated, noble cases and sizeable amounts rescued, SEAL 911 has only raised $200,000 in funds to their donation multisignature wallet address (at the time of writing) (Era.zksync .network, n.d.). The feeling is that supported projects quickly forget who was there to rescue them in their time of need once they are back up and running.

These dynamics highlight the dire need to improve blockchain white hat incentives across the industry to align interests in improving security. While ideological and reputational social norms encourage ethical hacking behaviours, the desire to maintain a good conscience or receive kudos on social media is not enough to ensure the sustainability of expert white hat security participation in the blockchain industry.

Referring to bug bounty programmes, Mitchell Amador, Founder/ CEO of the white hat hacker bug bounty platform Immunefi, states: 'It is not true that most security professionals are died-in-the-wool, hardcore-committed whitehats, and it's not true that people will just disclose if they find stuff. Incentives are crucial to making sure disclosures happen' (private communication, SEAL chat).

Another SEAL contributor remarked:

> I know several top talent whitehats with the skills to help, but aren't motivated by altruism. They need the potential financial reward to be involved. I've rarely seen bounties deter black hats, but we need more whitehats in the fight & pretending they're all motivated by public good is how government security fell behind big tech's.

Others responded in agreement with the '100' emoji, emphasising that everyone will have different moral compasses and financial goals, but the right mix of incentives are needed to align efforts.

Put simply in the chat by Josselin Feist (independent security researcher, former engineering director at security audit firm Trail of Bits), 'rewards attract people that focus on that money' (private communication, SEAL chat). In this context, incentives speak to expanding the number of people who might be motivated to protect a system, rather than reducing black hat activity. This dynamic acknowledges that there are different incentives for different characters who can contribute constructively to security.

As pcaversaccio expressed in the chat: 'I don't really care about money that much but about fairness and justice'. Fairness and justice in this context mean to have the ability 'to transact value of any form in a privacy-preserving, censorship-resistant and secure way'. Samczsun responded in agreement – highlighting that they choose to focus on building SEAL's pro bono infrastructure for security, rather than chasing bounties full time (which samczsun had done very successfully to earn him a widespread reputation as a blockchain white hat hacker before leading SEAL at a not-for-profit organisation) (private communication, SEAL chat).

'Scam survivor turned investigator' ZachXBT further demonstrates that pure altruism isn't enough to sustain the thousands of hours required to do good in blockchain security. They state in a post on X: 'One of my biggest regrets is not prioritizing making money', lamenting their lack of business sense in terms of ability to monetise their valuable skill set (ZachXBT, 2025a).

The response on X was astounding. To incentivise ZachXBT to continue their work, a memecoin developer donated 500 million coins to ZachXBT's public wallet address. What unfolded next on the public blockchain is that the pseudonymous investigator ZachXBT used the memecoin to create a liquidity pool which boosted the price of his own ZachXBT token, and then cashed out approximately $3.9 million through an over the counter (OTC) cryptocurrency trading desk.

The event sparked some controversy. Some critics claimed that ZachXBT executed a 'rug pull' on holders of his coin, stating on X: 'ZachXBT spent years conning brainlets from cryptotwitter into thinking he was some good guy investigator only to rug pull yall for $5M LMFAO' (Flock (6'3), 2025). Meanwhile, others argued that he took advantage of a random scammer sending him memecoins, and the money is in good hands, stating: 'Zach deserves far more money than this for what he's done for the space' (Foobar, 2025). In response to what they perceived as unfair criticisms, community members fundraised over $50,000 in donations and memecoins for ZachXBT to demonstrate continued support for his work (Mooose, 2025).

This incident underscores how blockchain white hat security is sustained by a hybrid economy of both altruism and financial incentive – where financial gain and community recognition coexist with a deeper ethos of collective responsibility and mutual aid. Unsolicited and often anonymous donations reflect a culture of giving back to those who protect the ecosystem. They suggest that ethical hacking and security efforts are often rewarded through gestures of gratitude rather than formal arrangements or contracts. Even so, donations often fall short of the true value contributed by the goodwill of volunteer blockchain white hat hackers, and concrete incentives are needed to ensure the sustainability of security efforts.

According to the co-founder and former CEO of Code4rena, the first competitive bug bounty platform that effectively gamified hacking, 'security researchers will follow the money' (Picnic, pers. communication, 2024). Yet, it is not always clear what the right level of incentives is. For example, a protocol called Euler Finance had undergone a security audit and was insured by a security firm called Sherlock. The protocol also offered a $1 million bug bounty – one of the largest in the industry at the time. Despite these measures, it was exploited for $200 million by a nineteen-year-old attacker who later returned the funds, reportedly out of guilt (and possibly fear of legal recourse) (Omniscia, 2023; Abrams, 2023). This raises the question: why was the $1 million bounty not claimed instead? This incident highlights the limitations of current incentive structures in blockchain security, demonstrating that even substantial bug bounties may fail to deter exploitative behaviour or encourage responsible disclosure.

Security dynamics are constantly evolving amidst the ever-evolving landscape of the blockchain industry. As Ethereum Foundation security representative, Fredrik Svantes, stated on a podcast, 'I think we are still behind when it comes to the protocol security stuff. I think we need to expand that because the more Ethereum grows, the more potential adversaries there's going to be' (Blockchain Security Series, 2024). The rise of automated bots and large language models (LLMs) only exacerbates this evolution. Many developers now use LLMs to write software code. This risks the creation of new threats, such as AI code poisoning, in which attackers inject malicious code into the underlying training data of AI models, which can then get utilised by developers coding with LLMs and pushed into production to exploit users. This has already occurred in the ecosystem of major blockchain Solana (Cos, 2024).

pcaversaccio pointed out in the chat how automation can contribute to 'front running' of transactions to win rewards for bot operators:[4] 'So most white hat labelled attacks nowadays are friendly MEV bots'.[5] pcaversaccio then pointed to the evolving nature of blockchain security coordination, stating: 'One of the reasons there are fewer real white hat hacks like in 2020 is due to bounty programs or SEAL 911 which enables efficient comms with projects instead of hacking it' (private communication, SEAL chat).

Addressing blockchain insecurity is not confined to the technical boundaries or operational responsibilities of any single protocol team, but instead relies on broader, ecosystem-wide collaboration, including from white hats. Incidents such as smart contract exploits or phishing campaigns often transcend individual platforms, affecting users, liquidity and trust across multiple protocols and chains. In these contexts, white hat actors play a critical role in identifying anomalies, mitigating damage and coordinating war rooms and responses across protocol teams, security providers, blockchain forensics and exchanges. Their interventions often require informal trust networks to efficiently mobilise on and off chain communications and the capacity to mobilise resources quickly, including the negotiation of bug bounties or freeze funds. This distributed form of security governance highlights the interdependence of actors in decentralised systems and the necessity of aligning incentives across diverse stakeholders to ensure effective and timely incident response. As such, blockchain security emerges as boundary work that extends beyond formal organisational boundaries, shaped by both technical coordination and the social infrastructure of reputation and reciprocity.

Conclusion

Blockchain security is a distributed and collective endeavour that depends on the coordination of diverse actors across the ecosystem. Such forms of decentralised security governance require more than individual ethics or ideological commitment. White hat activity illustrates how incident response, vulnerability disclosure and trust-building extend beyond the authority or capacity of any single protocol team and require boundary work, boundary objects and ecosystem-wide collaboration. Yet, incentives for white hats to participate proactively in blockchain security remain unstructured and retroactive or donation-based, and therefore are insufficient for system-wide sustainability.

The chapter that follows explores the developments occurring in blockchain security coordination and provision, specifically the social, technical, economic and legal infrastructure that SEAL is developing to align incentives, facilitate cooperation and support rapid response across a fragmented ecosystem. Together, these infrastructures and objects point toward a possible future where security is not only reactive but proactively designed into the ecosystem, enabling ethical hackers, developers and users to better defend the protocols they rely on.

Notes

1 Personal details retracted. Thank you to the brave author for agreeing to share this upsetting experience for the benefit of others.
2 Note: quoted material retains original spelling, punctuation and grammar.
3 See also Prisma Finance hack: Abrams, 2024.
4 Front-running is a type of exploit or manipulation in financial markets, including blockchain-based systems, where a party uses advance knowledge of a pending transaction to increase transaction fees and place their own transaction ahead of it in order to claim a profit. In the context of blockchain, especially in DeFi, front-running typically occurs when a malicious actor observes a large transaction waiting in the public mempool (the queue of unconfirmed transactions), and then submits their own transaction with a higher gas fee so that it is executed before the original one, allowing them to exploit price changes or arbitrage opportunities before the initial transaction is finalised.
5 A 'friendly MEV bot' is a searcher bot that engages in miner/maximal extractable value (MEV) strategies on a blockchain (usually Ethereum), usually to find arbitrage opportunities, but does so in a way that is non-exploitative, non-malicious and often beneficial to users, protocols or the broader network. For example, see: Reguerra, 2025.

4

The security alliance –
Infrastructure for security

Introduction

Security in decentralised systems relies not only on technical robustness, but also on the interaction of social, economic, legal and institutional arrangements that enable coordination across diverse actors and make insecurity legible. This chapter examines how security is collectively produced and governed in decentralised contexts, focusing on the infrastructures that enable coordination. Central to this exploration is the case of the Security Alliance (SEAL), a not-for-profit organisation dedicated to raising security capabilities across decentralised ecosystems. SEAL operates at the intersection of community building, process development and tooling to advance a set of initiatives that seek to address the technical, economic, social and legal dimensions of blockchain security. These include auditing and vulnerability disclosure programs, community education and threat intelligence sharing, policy and regulatory engagement and incentive mechanisms for security researchers and contributors. Situating SEAL within the wider context of decentralised modes of security governance and infrastructure provision, this chapter investigates how traditional institutional models are being adapted and applied to the demands of decentralised coordination. Particular attention is paid to the development of infrastructure for security as a means to address the complex dynamics of incentive alignment amidst the negotiation of risk, responsibility and reward among actors with divergent goals, capacities and time horizons. The approaches being pioneered in the blockchain security industry are predicated on the ongoing need to align as many stakeholders as possible to address the persistent state of insecurity.

Calling SEAL 911

When I checked my wallet, my cryptocurrency was gone.[1] What I needed was a white hat. With no one else to turn to, I logged in to the chat application Telegram. Typing in the handle '@seal_911_bot', I was hoping to contact the newly launched Security Alliance for one of the volunteer security expert 'Seals' to come to my aid. I didn't like my chances, being on Australia time, but I had heard that the channel was manned around the clock in shifts.

Under the leadership of the pseudonymous Founder/CEO and white hat hacker 'samczsun', the mission of SEAL is to 'serve the community' via a number of bespoke cybersecurity initiatives, to 'secure the future of crypto' (Security Alliance, n.d.a). SEAL 911 was a cornerstone initiative, providing a critical, free of charge emergency help line for projects and individuals. At the time, all I wanted was to secure my $573 USD worth of stable coins.

While most blockchain user security and ecosystem security has been reactive to black hat hacks and the tactics of scammers, SEAL 911 not only responds but takes a proactive security posture: 'Our actions involve identifying root causes, tracing stolen funds, pointing to resources on best practice responses, and recovering stolen social media accounts', stated one of the SEAL 911 responders during an interview.

Participation in cryptocurrency communities (such as DAOs) and activities (i.e. using protocols to better understand how they work) is a regular part of my research practice as a digital ethnographer. As such, I had signed up to take part in a DAO-led cryptocurrency grants donation round as an experiment to raise funds for open access research. My Ethereum cryptocurrency wallet was linked to an Ethereum Name System (ENS) domain in plain English, meaning that instead of typing in 0x0x143456439bfbc6bb.., people can type in, for example, *firstnamenickname.eth* to send funds to my account (kind of like a domain name address, but for a cryptocurrency account). However, someone had sneakily bought my domain name four months prior when it was up for renewal, and I hadn't checked or noticed. This meant that I could still share the address to receive funds but any funds deposited to that address were being redirected to the 'domain squatters'' wallet address and out of my control.

The first message when I opened the chat with @seal_911_bot read as follows:

What can this bot do?
    You can use this bot to contact SEAL 911, a team of volunteer security professionals, during emergency situations (smart contract hack, lost funds, critical bug, etc.)

I typed:

/start

Following some code of conduct details about privacy and information handling, the bot asked:

What is the nature of the emergency?
Do you have any relevant details?

Aware of respecting the SEAL 911 volunteers' time and given the high importance of other examples listed under each prompt, such as 'protocol hack', I began my request with: 'Low priority'.
    I shared the details of the incident and a link to the public record of transactions on the Ethereum blockchain, and a ticket was created for me. To my surprise, samczsun himself responded seventy-four minutes later.

Hi kelsie! Probably not much to do here unfortunately. No way for anyone to take over an ens name so the best you can do is just change it up or ask nicely for them to transfer it back.

'Asking nicely' involved sending a message to the squatter via the public blockchain to explain the situation and ask for it to be returned. This mode of communication is commonplace in ransom negotiations.

His kind and honest answer was expected. Losing oversight of the domain was my mistake and I felt like a newb (a 'newbie'). In the blockchain arena of self-custodianship where each individual is responsible for stewarding their own digital assets, I expected to be on my own. This incident could have happened to anyone. As per

Taylor Monahan ('Tayvano')'s statement on X, 'dear people who see stories abt [about] people who had their keys drained today or yesterday or tomorrow: please do not act like youre better and smarter than them. you aren't. they are already wildly aware they should've done something differently' (Tay, 2024b).

While SEAL couldn't do any more to help my case, their presence in the blockchain community is reshaping how 'security' is organised and rescuing millions of dollars across dozens and dozens of incidents (estimated at over $500 million as of August 2025).[2] Their initiatives provide a social layer of coordination that moves beyond traditional narratives of on-chain governance and accountability that rely exclusively on technical solutions, convening the patchwork of stakeholders and interfacing with law enforcement authorities to respond in crisis. The processes, tools and frameworks that SEAL has developed form a unique infrastructure for security: a decentralised, not-for-profit convened network of security experts, codes of conduct and norms about who can intervene, when and under what conditions. The sections that follow outline the nature and dynamics of SEAL's key initiatives.

SEAL 911: emergency response

SEAL 911 connects blockchain users and white hat hackers via a free 24/7 emergency reporting line for support with incident response, responsible vulnerability disclosure or other security issues. The reporting line is accessed via a Telegram bot, described in the 'calling SEAL 911' vignette above, and responded to by a volunteer team of top blockchain security contributors who can help triage, patch, recover and/or resolve incidents on both a personal and protocol level. Membership to the group of security expert responders is managed by SEAL by invitation only, and commercial organisations are capped in their representation in an attempt to maintain neutrality (pcaversaccio, 2024i).

SEAL 911 response coverage areas include core blockchain infrastructure (for example, software clients and exchanges),[3] applications, wallets and users across various blockchain ecosystems, including Ethereum, Solana and more. Contributions to the industry involve identifying root causes, tracing stolen funds, pointing to resources on best practice responses and recovering stolen social media accounts.

Attacks have been both pre-empted and halted by SEAL 911 responders. According to SEAL 911 team members, over $100 million of value in cryptocurrency tokens has been saved, and hundreds of support tickets have been actively responded to, with thousands received and triaged. Furthermore, numerous high-level, black hat on-chain negotiations have been conducted for the return of funds, or worse, the return of hostages (more on this in Chapter 6).

On August 7, 2024, pcaversaccio, lead of the SEAL 911 response team, posted on X:

> 1/ Exactly 1 year ago, we (=SEcurity ALliance; SEAL) launched a big and bold experiment: SEAL 911. In my words, it's 'The lifeline for emergencies' designed to connect with a small group of highly trusted security professionals in case of emergency. But enough cheap talk, so, what have we achieved in the past 365 days? – ~$100M USD saved (guesstimate including phishing prevention measures) – 916 tickets handled (78 in 2023 & 838 in 2024 so far) – Actively managed +100 war rooms – Blocked over +100k phishing domains – Built the best-in-class SEAL 911 team of 46 volunteers: https://github .com/security-alliance/seal-911. Give them a big shoutout because they selflessly help you' [followed by an image of a seal animal in commando gear]. (pcaversaccio, 2024d)

In one example, SEAL 911 helped lead the negotiations with a hacker, using on-chain messages to their cryptocurrency wallet address to strike a deal. This often involved narrating the black hat hacker as a white hat if they returned the funds and promising not to pursue further investigations and legal action against them. The message read:

> Thank you for working with us to return user funds. We are willing to move forward with this agreement, in the interest of making users whole. Send the funds to this address from which we are messaging you 0x52256ef863a713Ef349ae6E97A7E8f3578514555.Once the funds have arrived, we will tweet the whitehat announcement. You will then have 4 hours to return the remaining 40%. When this is fully resolved, we will disregard the information we have gathered and we can put this behind us. (Etherscan, 2024)

This negotiation resulted in over 90 per cent of the stolen funds being returned to a project called Dolomite (a margin trading protocol on the Arbitrum blockchain, a 'Layer 2' within the Ethereum ecosystem), labelling the hacker that exploited the protocol and stole funds as a white hat (Dolomite, 2024).

In another DeFi hack intervention, SEAL assisted in the negotiation of 100 per cent of funds being returned to users at the market value of $2.3 million in cryptocurrency tokens at the time (Socket Tech, 2024). One blockchain security auditing team reported on X: 'Today I messaged the SEAL911 hotline with a bug I found in production. 15 minutes later, the CEO of the project was informed. 50 minutes later, the code was patched and no longer exploitable. I cannot recommend SEAL911 enough' (Marco De Vries, 2023).

SEAL 911 solves a number of security coordination issues in the blockchain industry. It allows for incident reporting, responsible disclosure of vulnerabilities, coordination of multi-stakeholder war rooms during live incidents and hack recovery support for end users (with or without bounties) (pcaversaccio, 2023). pcaversaccio's thread on X continues:

Simply put: ping us for any emergency

- Vulnerability disclosure
- White hat rescue
- Hacker negotiations
- Ongoing exploit
- Phishing scam
- Pig butchering / Sha Zhu Pan
- Malware
- Account takeovers
- Fake wallets / extensions

If we don't have the right skills internally, we probably have the connections to people who do. (pcaversaccio, 2024c)

Negotiations focus on protecting users' assets in strict adherence to the SEAL 911 Code of Conduct regarding acting in the interests of the victims (see Chapter 3).

In one interaction between two SEAL 911 responders in the SEAL chat, they reflect on the public communications of a hacked protocol, stating:

> Contributor 1: 'tbh [to be honest] i dont agree with this and I told them
>
> I don't know for sure they can say "NO users were impacted"…
>
> like all good web3 security I assume they have done nothing but put everything back up and call it a day [a number of crying laughter emojis]'.
>
> Contributor 2: '"just yolo [you only live once] it" mindset
>
> whats the worst that can happen with millions of assets under management'
>
> Contributor 1 responded (sarcastically): 'we use SAFE [referring to the SAFE multisignature wallet Decentralised Application] its all good'
>
> Contributor 2: 'the unfortunate truth is that many would act the same'
>
> Contributor 1 retorted more sharply: '**fuck them […] it makes me so angry that people aren't careful with others funds, its substantial for some of them and you should do your god damn best to make sure they dont lost it from you being dumb' [eliciting multiple '100' emoji reactions in agreement from other SEALs in the chat channel].

This interaction emphasises the role of SEAL 911 responders, many of whom consider themselves white hats, across both developer and user sides of the ecosystem. While end users need to be more aware of clicking sign buttons to consent to transactions, 'Developers need to understand that they are developing mission-critical software and that smart contracts should be considered hardware rather than software in terms of security', stated pcaversaccio in an interview, referring to the fact that hardware is typically immutable once manufactured and deployed. Once smart contracts are deployed on-chain, they become difficult to update or change, which has numerous flow-on effects. These complex security dynamics warrant system testing, which is explored in the SEAL initiative that follows.

Wargames: blockchain red-teaming exercises

SEAL Wargames facilitate free practice security exercises with the goal of aiding teams to improve their security processes, as well as prepare for and prevent security exploits. Known as 'red-teaming', these exercises are a proactive security practice to test vulnerabilities and response measures. For the project participating in a red-teaming exercise, SEAL's Wargame process includes engagement with a protocol team, background research to understand the target protocol, a tabletop exercise to plan the simulation, a window of time in which the simulated attack will occur in a simulated operating environment to test the protocol team's response and a post-mortem. Wargames exercises take dozens of hours to prepare for, with the team doing deep research on security vulnerabilities and then building infrastructure to create realistic scenarios. These simulation exercises provide an adversarial perspective that helps uncover weaknesses, ideally before they can be exploited by malicious actors.

With an emphasis on Wargames 'post-mortems' (incident reports), the SEAL team observes how a protocol team responds, and then works with them to identify areas for improvement. The SEAL team places a heavy emphasis on incident communications and process improvement to develop a culture of vigilance and socialise best practice approaches across projects.

Engaging in red-teaming exercises across the ecosystem equips stakeholders with the knowledge, skills, practice and networks needed to respond to real threats. Once an exercise has been run, a project retains open communication channels with the SEAL community in the event of clarification, information sharing, or crisis. On numerous occasions, security teams subsequently reached out to SEAL for advice on real security events for advice.

SEAL x Yearn: attack simulation

One Wargames attack simulation I was involved in was with the elite security team of major DeFi protocol 'Yearn'. In preparation for the Yearn DeFi protocol Wargames attack simulation, the SEAL team stated in the chat: 'take this Yearn Plane down!', followed by an aeroplane emoji and multiple fire emojis.

It was 12:01 PM EST on September 20, 2023, when Wargames initiative lead Isaac Patka posted in the war room on Telegram that the simulation had begun:

> Welcome to the SEAL Wargames Team's Simulation War Room.
>
> You're now part of a real-time exercise set in the Yearn ecosystem. Your mission involves diagnosing and responding to a simulated incident as if it were real and the stakes were high. In other words, do everything you would normally do, including triaging, patching, and (simulating) communicating with the public. After the simulation is complete, you'll have a chance to go over how you did and where room for improvement might be found...
>
> Good luck. The simulation is about to begin.

This message marked the second SEAL Wargames attack simulation on a major DeFi protocol by the SEAL Wargames Team, which I was involved in as an observer, calendar scheduler and default note-taker. More broadly, it marked an effort to shift the security landscape of the cryptocurrency ecosystem and presented insights into how formal and informal security mechanisms are developed in open-source, permissionless infrastructure.

The players on the blue team (a.k.a. good guys) included a bunch of core contributors to the DeFi protocol Yearn, including Storm0x, FP, Poolpi Tako, wavey, dudesahn, Val, banteg, Spalen and Rare Weasel. My access to observe the simulation had been granted by the red team attackers: samczsun and the coordinator of the simulation, Isaac Patka. Over eighty hours of work had gone into preparing and developing the scenario, including tooling, a bot-enabled notification channel and 'meme' joke ads to distract the security team as they worked to respond under pressure. Now, the simulation had begun.

The first Yearn team member to respond was dudesahn, sharing 'Lmao wait it's starting at the earliest possible time? [...] I'm eating lunch so will be a bit slow for a few mins [laughing emoji]'. As the team spun up a voice channel to be able to talk and type at the same time, we were viewing a simulation of a number of Yearn vaults, and all had access to a second Telegram channel that was pinging us with incessant notifications with price updates from the open-source block explorer BlockScout, Yearn vault liquidity reports and an 'Arb' (arbitrage) Profit Report. Within moments, the Yearn team started to diagnose the situation, stating:

> 'Okay so clearly ETH price is being manipulated'.
> dudesahn asked, 'Where is this eth price being reported from?'.
> Poolpi tako replied, 'Compound oracle'.
> dudesahn said, 'OK. So someone is attacking compound and it's basically fucking us over'.

The strategy of the attack was to manipulate the Compound oracle price, borrow USDC against that, and extract funds from the protocol.

By 12.03 PM, Storm0x had posted an urgent status report indicating an issue with Compound, mentioning the affected vaults and suggesting some strategies to mitigate the damage before halting the attack. They posted: 'GOAL try to minimize damage impact, and assess if we need to take immediate action'. Pulling out an emergency procedure card, Val shared a link, and Storm0x stressed the importance of setting the deposit limit to zero. After some negotiation around the correct multisignature wallet-based governance process they could follow with the participants present (without needing to wake up anyone else from a different time zone), the team agreed that they had quorum to sign a transaction.

Before signing, the Yearn team's priority was to simulate the steps on a 'fork' (copy of software) in a local operating environment to confirm the strategy would allow them to safely exit. Thirty-four minutes into the simulation, the team was clear on the transactions affected in the vault, knew that it was an issue with Compound, and had identified the need to minimise damage and assess immediate actions.

> Looking at their manuals, Poolpi asked 'would emergency shut down do this?', then continued, 'we have never used it in the past'.
>
> Val asked FP, 'would you recommend collat target = 0 and tend, or emegencyShutdown?'.
>
> Storm0x asked, 'can we get a simulation in local rpc [remote procedure call] to check that the steps are safe and we can delever?',

referring to the 'unwidening' of strategy so it withdraws from the underlying protocols and returns funds it 'borrowed' from the DeFi vault.

In response, dudesahn reflected the general sentiment by warning 'we're not fucked yet but we will be if we fail to withdraw'.

At precisely thirty-seven minutes into the exercise, not only was the vulnerability identified but a strategy was in place. After testing the command, the team decided they had quorum from multisig signers that they had called (including waking some up in the middle of the night) and were happy to run this command. The command initiated an emergency exit mode, a 'set of actions that seek to unwind and divest funds back to the Vault as quickly and smoothly as possible, with as minimal losses as possible'. The total time to safe harbour assets and declare it was fifty-six minutes, with Storm0x announcing in the chat 'FUNDS ARE SAFU!! we are out from compound'.

Upon debrief, the SEAL red team declared that Yearn's effort was 'impressive', particularly their use of pre-prepared emergency manuals. Their performance could now be reviewed and updated to reflect learnings from the exercise. The Yearn team responded rapidly and identified that the root cause of the attack was a dependency on a price oracle and not an issue with their code. They also acknowledged they could have done some things better, particularly the time taken to action the emergency exit mode to limit new deposits. In a normal scenario with the standard tooling available (rather than a custom-built simulation environment), the response would have been even faster. Part of the immediate debrief procedure included consideration of if, and how, such a situation would be publicly communicated and reported on, including timestamps from the event. In the case of Yearn, a public disclosure policy is in place, which they have had to enact multiple times in the past (including on hacks of $15 million in crypto tokens) (Yearn, n.d.; Malwa, 2020).

Although conducted as a very serious exercise, the simulation also featured compulsory memes for fun – characteristic of hacker playfulness, or as they say, for the 'lulz'. The 'fork' of Blockscout that was used in the simulation exercise to explore blocks on the blockchain included joke advertisements created by SEAL team

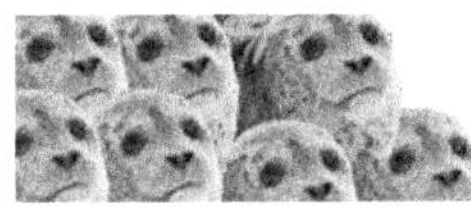

Figure 4.1 'SEALS 4 SALE' joke advertisement by David Desjardins

member David Desjardins to replace PayPal marketing, including a banner with seal heads on the left, and 'seals 4 sale' heading on the right with subtitle 'Find your certified pre-owned seal at www.seals2sale.com'.

According to Isaac, simulations push teams to up their detection game and relentlessly 'mitigate, then resolve' security-related matters. SEAL adds social resiliency to protocols. Attack simulations not only help a protocol to better prepare for unforeseen scenarios but also encourage teams to consider the issues that come with composable infrastructure, the cascade effects of how contagion in one protocol can spread and how to communicate across protocol teams to coordinate responses (either in a simulation or in a live situation) via the (optional and non-exclusive) SEAL 911 disclosure service. After the Yearn simulation, Isaac offered in the chat, 'If anyone wants to contribute to future attack scenarios and doomsday scenarios, feel free'. SEAL have run 'attack sims' with numerous other major protocols, including Compound, Optimism and Coinbase, and have a waitlist of others to follow.

While SEAL 911 and SEAL Wargames aim to enhance blockchain security through social means, SEAL also engages in initiatives informed by legal and economic approaches to incentivise both blockchain projects and hackers to improve blockchain security.

SEAL Safe Harbor: legal assurances for white hats

The Whitehat Safe Harbor Legal Agreement (SEAL Safe Harbor) is a legal template that can be enshrined on-chain to clarify the legal terms, conditions and processes for security researchers to aid in rescuing funds during an active exploit (Security Alliance, n.d.b). The initiative marked a key grand gesture of coordination for SEAL, who worked across major blockchain foundations for highly sought after blockchain lawyers, venture capitalists and security experts to shape a legal agreement that would enable a priori agreement for legitimate white hat engagement when a protocol was under active exploit – addressing the significant barrier to security of white hat liability.

SEAL Safe Harbor provides a contractual framework for white hat hackers to intervene in the event of exploits or security breaches affecting blockchain projects. As a legal agreement drafted by numerous blockchain law experts, it establishes the responsibilities of white hat hackers, providing clear guidelines for the responsible disclosure of vulnerabilities and the procedures for fund recovery efforts. At the same time, the agreement outlines the blockchain community's commitment to ensuring legal immunity and financial rewards for the successful intervention of white hats.

The aim of SEAL Safe Harbor is to ensure that the actions of white hats are conducted within legal and ethical boundaries, and to protect them from adverse legal actions when engaging in funds rescues (which often require exploiting a protocol to hack funds faster than a black hat). According to Kurt Opsahl, SEAL contributor and Associate General Counsel for Cybersecurity and Civil Liberties Policy at Filecoin Foundation, 'Finding vulnerabilities and fixing vulnerabilities requires a legal environment that makes that possible' (DeFi Security Summit, 2024c).

In doing so, the agreement reduces legal uncertainty for civil actions between a protocol and white hat hacker to encourage engagement if the hacker believes they are skilled enough to respond effectively to a live exploit. It also aligns incentives as protocol teams can pre-agree to provide a percentage of the bounty for rescued funds. Additionally, the funds are routed via a SEAL wallet address to ensure the bounty is actually paid to the white hat in the case of a successful rescue. This is known as the Asset Recovery Address (ARA), which serves as a designated destination for funds recovered during security interventions, providing white hat hackers with a mechanism to collect a portion of the restored funds as a reward for their efforts. By sending funds to the ARA smart contract, white hat hackers can be assured that they will be able to claim a predetermined percentage (typically 10 per cent) of the recovered assets, as stipulated in the terms of the agreement.

The main terms of the agreement are as follows:

- White hats who act competently and in good faith, and return all rescued funds to an ARA, (1) will be protected from legal action and not face legal liability for their rescue actions that may initially take user funds from a protocol, and (2) may receive a prespecified reward for the funds rescue.
- The SEAL Safe Harbor applies only during *active* exploits: white hats cannot initiate a funds removal process from a protocol.
- If a white hat engages proactively via a conscious decision, they will be considered a *prospective* white hat; if a bot someone owns or operates engages in the rescue, the owner of the bot will be considered a *retrospective* white hat.
- The white hat may claim rewards through a public message about where the reward should be sent after returning funds to the ARA or by retaining the specified portion of the recovered funds when returning funds to the ARA. This is at the discretion of the development team – not the white hat.
- White hats agree to certain conditions, including but not limited to avoiding collateral damage, the DevCo/foundation for the protocol will be the ones to determine whether you've abided by the Agreement, and you are not a sanctioned individual (known bad actor) and are otherwise complying with all laws (Security Alliance, n.d.b).

Along with meeting requirements to avoid conflicts of interest and Office of Foreign Assets Control (OFAC) sanctions, the white hat must be able to answer 'yes' to a checklist of conditions, including:

- Is this an active, urgent exploit?
- Are you unable to responsibly disclose the exploit (e.g. via a bug bounty program) due to time constraints or other reasons?
- Can you reasonably expect your intervention to be net beneficial, reducing total losses to the protocol and associated entities?
- Are you experienced and confident in your ability to manage execution risk, avoiding unintentional loss of funds?
- Will you avoid intentionally profiting from the exploit in any way other than through the reward granted by the protocol?
- Have you confirmed the agreement has been duly adopted by the protocol community? (Security Alliance, n.d.b)

Enough DeFi protocols have adopted The Whitehat Safe Harbor Legal Agreement to cover more than $20 billion in cryptocurrency on-chain token asset value as of August 2025 (Security Alliance, 2025a). This marks well over 10 per cent of Total Value Locked in blockchain DeFi protocols (Security Alliance, 2025b).

The Safe Harbor Agreement provides the legal and economic infrastructure to ensure a level of certainty in white hat engagements for both protocols and hackers, where previously there was only 'good faith' that a white hat would be recognised as such, rather than being pursued in legal recourse for hacking a protocol. The a priori agreement establishes a clear process for stakeholders to follow in the case of emergency, as another example of a pre-emptive, rather than reactive, security measure. Furthermore, it demonstrates an example of institutional adaptation, where legal measures of accountability and enforcement have been adapted to a decentralised context, while maintaining the spirit of decentralised governance in how actions among distributed actors are coordinated. Aiming to complement other security measures (such as audits, processes and bug bounty programmes), the Safe Harbor team intends to incentivise white hat behaviour throughout the blockchain ecosystem.

SEAL INTEL

Among other SEAL projects (including anti-phishing bots and scam databases) is the SEAL INTEL (intelligence) initiative, which actively manages SEAL-ISAC. The term ISAC stands for 'Information Sharing and Intelligence Center'. An ISAC is a platform for real-time inter-organisational information sharing and collaboration. ISACs are used across various industries to share intelligence about threat actors and enhance cybersecurity resilience. SEAL-ISAC is based on the original Financial Services ISAC (FS-ISAC); an international, seven-thousand-member, not-for-profit industry consortium dedicated to reducing cyber-risk in the financial system (FS-ISAC, n.d.). Typically, ISACs are trusted entities that collect, analyse and disseminate actionable threat information to their members, as well as providing members with tools to mitigate risks. The initial FS-ISAC was founded in 1999 as a response to a Presidential Directive from the US government. Yet, SEAL-ISAC has adapted this model to become 'crypto native' by gathering, 'analyzing, and disseminating blockchain and cryptocurrency threat intelligence' (Security Alliance, n.d.c). SEAL-ISAC gathers data feeds about blockchain security from relevant providers (e.g. wallets and exchanges) to build a valuable platform that is open to reputable members, and has built a community of security stakeholders that can utilise that data.

'What is different about SEAL is their ability to get the right people, in the right place, at the right time', stated one contributor in a team call. Leading not through talk but by 'shipping' (a.k.a. building software), the threat intelligence platform, SEAL is focusing on engineering and infrastructure support.

The types of stakeholders that are members of SEAL-ISAC include cryptocurrency exchanges and trading platforms; blockchain development projects and platforms; wallet providers and crypto storage solutions; mining pools and infrastructure providers; cybersecurity firms and researchers specialising in blockchain and cryptocurrency; and regulatory experts and bodies interested in or working with cryptocurrency projects.

Given the unique challenges and the rapidly evolving nature of blockchain technology and digital assets, SEAL-ISAC focuses on the specific needs and vulnerabilities of the cryptocurrency sector, including those surfaced by SEAL 911. With more money flowing into the market, the types of threats that the SEAL 911 team observes are blockchain-specific and ever-evolving.

According to one of the SEAL 911 expert white hat hackers, the majority of tickets are phishing scams (people losing their cryptocurrency tokens via malicious approvals and compromised private keys) and romance scams that involve investing in cryptocurrency (known as 'pig butchering' scams). The remainder are responsible disclosures by other white hats regarding potential vulnerabilities (such as re-entrancy attacks where there is a bug in smart contract code and access control issues) or projects reaching out for help once hacked.

While traditional ISACs generally charge membership fees, and a number of crypto security firms try to monetise intelligence sharing products and services, SEAL-ISAC membership was intentionally planned to be completely free.

'Although there are more players to coordinate in a decentralized ecosystem like cryptocurrency, there are even higher incentives to collaborate on industry-wide security to protect users from having their funds drained, to mitigate cascade effects from hacks, and to improve the reputation of the industry', stated Ryan Wenger, the initial lead of SEAL-ISAC.

Infrastructure and incentives for security

In an interview, pcaversaccio stated:

> People need to understand what it means to hit a 'confirm' button in this area, moreover, developers need to understand that they are developing mission-critical software and that smart contracts should be considered hardware rather than software in terms of security.
>
> SEAL is still a big experiment trying to lay the groundwork for white hat work, protocol security and the point of contact for help [note, this quote was collected in early 2024, and the organisation has since matured]. SEAL is helping in the best possible way: we act, we move, we try and experiment, we give hope. Simply put: we get shit done. SEAL shows that it is possible for the best security experts working for competing organisations to join forces and work together for a more secure future. So we're showing that collaboration indeed works. Will the Safe Harbour Agreement work? I don't know. What will SEAL 911 look like in a year's time? I don't know. What I do know, however, is that some fundamental work has already been done that can be further developed and adapted to the market over time. We can now be proactive and not just reactive.
>
> Overall, security is much more about the mindset than anything else. It's the same in web2 or web3. (ethnographic interview)

Despite its achievements in mobilising largely voluntary contributions and donation-based funding across the ecosystem, significant challenges remain in ensuring the long-term sustainability of security provision. This was demonstrated in the following interaction in the SEAL chat regarding voluntary donation-based financial support from the community for a specific SEAL initiative (rather than donations to the overall not-for-profit organisation, of which named donors are recognised on the SEAL website):

'How are donations doing for seal911?' asked AndrewMohawk. pcaversaccio replied:

You can see them in our multisig [...] Around 95k since we started in Aug 2023 (to put that in perspective, we saved around 75m in 2024 alone). I could now write a long rant how people/projects forget very fast who helped them in their worst hours [...] I'm doing this since I'm intrinsically motivated to help this space, but too many hypocrites around (yes also in this group). But hey, don't hate the player, hate the game.

In another comment on X, pcaversaccio expressed:

We're fucking drowning in SEAL 911 tickets every damn day, with people getting drained left and right. It's brutal, and the reality is we're nowhere near fixing this. The harsh truth? Most of these tickets are coming from basic web2 issues – phishing, malware, the usual bullshit. No amount of smart contract audits is going to save these people. This is the biggest security nightmare our industry faces currently. (pcaversaccio, 2024h)

In contrast to traditional digital environments, where security consequences typically reflect on a centralised authority or responsible person, decentralised systems require novel institutional arrangements capable of aligning incentives across a heterogeneous set of actors. SEAL's proactive initiatives across social, technical, legal and economic margins reveal the need to align stakeholders across a decentralised ecosystem using all incentives possible to address the insecurity of the blockchain ecosystem. In this context, security is provisioned via infrastructure, social norms and relationships. Addressing insecurity requires fostering a culture of collaboration grounded in information sharing, coordinated response, responsible vulnerability disclosure and support for white hat practices. This culture of collaboration involves reciprocal arrangements of trust and reputation, as well as clear rules and channels of engagement. It also involves shifting towards a pre-emptive security posture that is self-aware of vulnerabilities and seeking continuous improvement. Within this landscape, SEAL cultivates legitimacy and trust not through formal authority but through its conduct, transparency and consistent support of projects and people. Its credibility as a good-faith actor is earned through reputation, adherence to its articulated code of conduct and demonstrable contributions to the broader ecosystem.

Conclusion

This chapter has examined how security is collectively coordinated within decentralised technology communities, with particular emphasis on the initiatives, infrastructure, norms and practices of SEAL. It has investigated the forms of cross-industry collaboration required to enhance security across decentralised digital ecosystems, highlighting how SEAL's work spans and integrates multiple regulatory modalities (i.e. social, technical, legal and economic). These initiatives transcend individual protocols or organisations, enabling collective insight and coordinated responses to emergent threats and systemic vulnerabilities, and elevating the role of the blockchain white hat hacker to one that is credible, necessary and celebrated. This chapter has shown that security infrastructure in decentralised systems is not merely technical, but fundamentally socio-technical, cultural and shaped by new forms of institutional imagination, coordination and conduct. The following chapter turns to the systemic challenges involved in provisioning and governing decentralised security at scale, examining how such efforts unfold across the broader blockchain industry.

Notes

1 Note. this vignette was originally published by Nabben and De Filippi in Flood and Robb (eds), Forthcoming.
2 An 'incomplete' SEAL 911 Incident Resolution log is available here: 'SEAL 911 Incident Resolution Log', GitHub, https://github.com/security-alliance/seal-911/blob/main/ACTIVITY.md
3 A software client is a piece of software that provides an application with a gateway to interact with the blockchain.

Part III

Decentralised digital security at scale

5

Decentralised security at scale – The geopolitics of blockchain security

Introduction

This chapter moves beyond individual hacks and exploits to examine how decentralised security operates at scale, with a focus on the intersection between cryptocurrency security and the geopolitics of blockchain infrastructure. It interrogates physical security, organised crime and state-backed actors – particularly the North Korea-linked Lazarus Group – as they target decentralised finance systems. By tracing how these Advanced Persistent Threat (APT) actors exploit blockchain technologies for illicit purposes, it reveals the broader implications for global security and policy. In doing so, this chapter shows how geopolitical tensions increasingly manifest through digital infrastructures, shaping the vulnerabilities, responses and power dynamics that characterise the insecurity of blockchain ecosystems today. In doing so, it shows how blockchain systems function as geopolitical battlegrounds where sovereignty, accountability and security are contested and coordinated.

Kidnappers, a ransom and a finger

January 24, 2025

Each morning, I opened the Security Alliance (SEAL) chat with expectations and apprehensions of what it could contain. On this particular day, I didn't expect to read about a crypto hostage situation where someone's finger had been cut off.

'These guys has no fucking clue what they are doing', said SEAL 911 incident response contributor Taylor Monahan. Her point was that they behaved like amateurs with little idea of how to launder the ransom money from cryptocurrency into cash. Their ransom funds were traced when they swapped ETH to USDT and subsequently frozen.

After further expressions of frustration, she continued: 'The problem is those are the worst kind bc they might be stupid enough to kidnap someone…Smart rational people don't kidnap people'.

pcaversaccio responded a few comments later: 'to be clear the investigation is still ongoing but people are safe'.

One SEAL responded in the thread: 'Did they return the finger', with the emoji of a monkey covering its eyes.

pcaversaccio responded in a far more serious tone: 'I'm not gonna answer this sorry', before presumably disappearing back into important white hat activities.

Giving voice to the general sentiment, another SEAL voiced: 'I'm in awe. and a bit of shock. You people are incredible'.

What had transpired is terrifying for anyone with, or perceived to have, access to digital currency. The co-founder of popular cryptocurrency hardware wallet company Ledger – which makes physical devices for self-storing cryptocurrency assets – and his wife were kidnapped from their home in France by a criminal gang. Each was taken to separate addresses and subsequently tortured for forty-eight hours while kidnappers demanded a ransom from the other Ledger co-founder (Sandor, 2025). The hostage victims were later rescued by elite tactical French police units and nearly all of the cryptocurrencies that were paid to the kidnappers were traced, frozen and seized (Le Monde, 2025). The crack response team responsible for on-chain efforts was assembled by the co-founder and former CTO of Ledger, including lawyers and SEAL 911.

'It's been an absolutely wild week', stated pcaversaccio on X. In a tone of justice akin to Batman, he continued: 'My deepest gratitude goes to the Ledger Co-Founders for trusting us (= SEAL 911) to assist with handling this highly sensitive case. Over 90% of the ransom funds are already frozen, and we're determined to hit 100%. Let this be a reminder – crime doesn't pay' (pcaversaccio, 2025).

SEAL contributors were pleased because they received public shout outs for their involvement in the rescue. For example, one article interviewed Ledger co-founder Nicolas Bacca, who called the overall response 'a unique organisational model for intervening in cryptocurrency ransom' (Raymond, 2025; Bacca, 2025a; Bacca, 2025b), specifically praising the efficient work of SEAL and sharing a link for people to donate to their work. Bacca observed that while coordination between parties – such as exchanges, legal teams and security experts – can be improved, this collaborative model has the potential to accelerate law enforcement responses globally and contribute to the development of an international standard. The case underscores the sobering and increasingly geopolitical nature of digital security within the cryptocurrency industry.

Later that same day of the Ledger security incident, pcaversaccio posted a screenshot of the Ledger Nano X OnChain web page in the SEAL chat. The site advertises Ledger on a physical key chain, with a product description as follows: 'Peace of mind you can wear. Security is a flex. So, secure your assets and wear them in style' (Ledger, n.d.).

pcaversaccio commented below the captured image, 'as a heads-up, I'm trying to push to ledger now (I think the timing is good now...[given the abduction]) to change how they sell their products, because that's not really how you should advertise it; not sure I succeed tho'. Multiple SEALs respond with the sideways laughing and tears emoji at the foolishness of publicly advertising that you own cryptocurrency by wearing it around your neck.

Digital frontiers become physical threats

Cybersecurity is increasingly recognised as a critical frontier of geopolitical contestation (DeNardis, 2014). These are not merely technical domains but strategic arenas in which states and non-state actors assert power, negotiate influence and project sovereignty. Cryptographic infrastructure – once confined to military and intelligence applications – now underpins global financial systems, communication networks and decentralised technologies, placing it at the heart of contemporary geopolitical struggles (Monsees, 2021). Cybersecurity breaches, state-sponsored attacks and the weaponisation of cryptographic tools further illustrate how digital infrastructures have become both targets and instruments in geopolitical rivalries. In particular, cryptocurrency has emerged as a site of geo-political conflict between nation-states (Hwang, 2023).

In late 2024, independent crypto crime investigator ZachXBT posted in his Telegram channel:

> Have seen an uptick in irl [in real life] robberies targeting crypto traders located in Western Europe over the past few months. The cases all involve known people in the crypto community where they were held at gunpoint. As the rest of the cycle continues be extra mindful of who you share your wins with and meet up with irl. (Zach XBT, personal communication)

Similarly, the US Attorney's Office published lists of people charged for over $263 million in organised cryptocurrency thefts, including home break-ins. The press release states:

> Database hackers hacked websites and servers to obtain cryptocurrency-related databases or purchased databases on the darkweb. Organizers and target identifiers organized and collated information across the databases to determine the most valuable targets. Callers cold-called victims and used social engineering to convince them their accounts were the subject of cyberattacks and the enterprise callers were attempting to help secure their accounts. Money launderers received the stolen crypto currency and turned it into fiat U.S. currency in the form of bulk cash or wire transfers. (US Attorney's Office District of Colombia, 2025).

Crypto crime presents a severe challenge for everyday users to remain vigilant against.

Physical security is dead

Hardware plays a foundational role in the cryptocurrency ecosystem. From mining rigs to hardware wallets (such as Ledger), physical devices are essential for maintaining blockchain network integrity and securing digital assets. Mining operations, which validate and secure transactions, rely on specialised hardware like Application-Specific Integrated Circuits (ASICs) and high-performance Graphics Processing Units (GPUs). These devices perform the intensive computations required by Proof of Work consensus mechanisms, making them vital to network security yet also susceptible to supply chain vulnerabilities.

The aim of hardware wallets is to add an extra layer of protection for those storing cryptocurrency by securing private keys offline, thereby reducing exposure to malware and remote attacks. Unlike software wallets, which remain 'hot' (internet connected) and thus more vulnerable to cyber exploits, hardware wallets require physical interaction – such as pressing a button on the device – to authorise transactions. This physical verification mechanism enhances security by limiting the attack surface accessible to hackers.

Additionally, the integration of technical techniques such as secure enclaves and Trusted Execution Environments (TEEs) into consumer hardware introduces further safeguards (There.Is.Now. Alternative, 2024). These measures aim to ensure that cryptographic operations are carried out in isolated, tamper-resistant environments. However, as highlighted by discussions in the SEAL chat, some people remained sceptical, declaring that 'physical security is dead'.

In late 2024, chat threads about privacy had emerged in the SEAL chat. AndrewMohawk posed the question to Zaki Manian (former contributor to Cosmos blockchain and co-founder of Iqlusion, an open-source hardware security solution): 'how do you see the future of privacy in the crypto space as it moves into more commonplace activities?'

Zaki responded: 'The main thing I would say is privacy in meatspace is pretty much completely dead. Patterns of life information is widely available from Tesla's and other senor equipped cars, ring doorbell cameras, license plate readers etc.'. Others concurred by tagging the message with the 100 emoji. The conversation flowed into reflections on privacy in encrypted devices, messages and financial transactions. AndrewMohawk and Zaki viewed encryption as a last-ditch effort to secure information that is revealed in metadata anyway, making privacy nearly impossible.

The sentiment that physical security is dead was reflected on posts on X, warning that a critical vulnerability was found in Chinese microchips used in some Bitcoin wallets (Protos, 2025). Tayvano responded in a thread on X that fundamental flaws in the hardware supply chain are insignificant anyway, in light of poor user behaviour, stating: 'it would be super cool if this actually mattered tbh. but ~0% of you actually use a hardware wallet and ~100% of those who do saved your secret recovery phrase to your hot af device(s) stop it lol' (Tay, 2025a).

DanielVF contributed to the conversation, sharing a link that read: 'Twelve Defendants Sentenced for Violent Home Invasion Robberies to Steal Cryptocurrency' (US Department of Justice, 2024). The article read, 'According to court documents and evidence presented at the trial…co-conspirators stole over $3.5 million from victims through SIM swapping and violent home invasions in which they held victims at gunpoint, assaulted them and bound them with plastic cable ties'.

'Got the books thrown at them', replied Tayvano. 'Though a lot seem to be gangbangers tbh. I think just the main 2 guys were doing both crypto and physical attacks'.

Even the FBI is employing hybrid digital–physical strategies to combat crypto-related crime, including the creation and operation of 'digital criminal organisations' as a means of infiltrating illicit networks (Ropek, 2025). In one case, the FBI took control of a dark web money-laundering service, 'ElonmuskWHM', and ran it for nearly a year (Ropek, 2025). The service enabled cybercriminals to cash out cryptocurrency obtained through illicit means. Ultimately, the operator was arrested and sentenced, and the proceeds of crime were seized. As FBI Special Agent in Charge Michael E. Stansbury stated:

> Gone are the days when cyber criminals, who enable and profit from the horrendous criminal conduct of others, can sit safely in their dens, across oceans, convinced of the limited reach of justice. The success of this operation proves that the FBI can unmask even the most careful anonymous online actors. (US Attorney's Office, Eastern District of Kentucky, 2025)

In another operation, the FBI created a fake cryptocurrency, called 'NexFundAI', as part of an investigation into pump-and-dump schemes. The Securities and Exchange Commission subsequently charged three market makers and nine individuals for allegedly manipulating the prices of certain crypto assets. In parallel, the Department of Justice brought the first ever criminal charges against financial services firms for market manipulation and 'wash trading' in the cryptocurrency sector, charging eighteen individuals and entities (US Securities and Exchange Commission, 2024; US Attorney's Office, District of Massachusetts, 2024).

Unfortunately for the cryptocurrency industry, threats extend beyond criminal gangs, hardware vulnerabilities or the reach of US law enforcement. As state-sponsored actors, such as North Korea's Lazarus Group, increasingly target cryptocurrency users and institutions, hardware security becomes both a critical line of defence and a potential vector of exploitation within broader cybersecurity threats.

Decentralised security at scale

North Korean cyber warfare

'Now you need to get really really scared', warned Peter Kacherginsky (Blockthreat crypto security newsletter editor/former Coinbase security) during his presentation at 'DeFi' (Decentralised Finance) Security Summit (DSS) in Bangkok. The slide behind him read 'APTs' (referring to Advanced Persistent Threats).

An APT is a prolonged and targeted threat to cybersecurity, where attackers attempt to compromise systems through unauthorised, often undetected access to steal sensitive data and/or funds (Baker, 2025).[1] Such threats are typically carried out by well-resourced groups, often backed by nation-states and involve sophisticated techniques like social engineering and software vulnerability exploits.

'If you are targeted by these guys, there is not much you can do', Kacherginsky stated. They are very sophisticated, operate as a team of a few thousand people and have successfully stolen hundreds of millions of dollars. 'If they want to hack you, they will. Is it about being slightly harder to hack then others, so they target them first'.

The 'serious villains' that Peter referred to in his presentation include the North Korean state-sponsored Lazarus Group and 'ATP38' (a name by the US Government as an umbrella term to represent several state-sponsored threat groups, including HIDDEN COBRA, Diamond Sleet, Labyrinth Chollima, TEMP, Hermit and Black Artemis) (CISA, 2022).

The Democratic People's Republic of Korea (DPRK) has built a computer network exploitation capability over the past ten years, enabling North Korea to steal billions of dollars in cryptocurrency, steal sanctioned information and generate revenue through IT work. While little is known about the complex and hierarchical inner workings of these groups, the US Cybersecurity and Infrastructure Agency (CISA) states that North Korea's cyber programmes 'pose a sophisticated and agile espionage, cybercrime, and attack threat' that has matured and is 'fully capable of achieving a variety of strategic objectives against diverse targets' – they are a threat to global cybersecurity (CISA, n.d.). Their tools and tactics include social engineering, malware injection, disruption, espionage (stealing intelligence) and sanctions evasion.

Lazarus Group's operations trace back to the mid-2000s. In 2014, they hacked Sony Pictures Entertainment (SPE) to retaliate against the imminent release of a satirical film that mocked DPRK's leader (*The Interview*). The conspirators gained access to SPE's network by sending malware to SPE employees. This was done via 'spear phishing messages', which often mimic a recruitment proposition and offer high-paying jobs to entice the recipients to download malware-laced cryptocurrency applications, a practice the US government refers to as 'TraderTraitor' (CISA, 2022). Once they gained access, the Lazarus Group stole confidential data, threatened SPE executives and employees and damaged thousands of computers. The event garnered a statement of reprimand from then US President Obama, thrusting the group into the global spotlight as an APT (White, 2022).

The Lazarus Group's operations include high-profile incidents such as the 2016 Bangladesh Bank heist, in which they attempted to steal nearly $1 billion in fiat currency via fraudulent SWIFT transactions, as well as the 2017 WannaCry ransomware attack, which disrupted computer systems around the world (US Department of Justice, 2018). Since then, the group has evolved into one of the most sophisticated state-backed cyber units, targeting government agencies, cryptocurrency platforms, media organisations, traditional financial institutions and defence sectors. US officials allege that the funds stolen by Lazarus are used to finance North Korea's ballistic missile and nuclear weapons programmes. In 2019, the US Department of the Treasury's Office of Foreign Assets Control

(OFAC) imposed sanctions on North Korean cyber groups responsible for attacks on critical infrastructure. 'Treasury is taking action against North Korean hacking groups that have been perpetrating cyber-attacks to support illicit weapon and missile programs', said Sigal Mandelker, Treasury Under Secretary for Terrorism and Financial Intelligence. 'We will continue to enforce existing US and UN sanctions against North Korea and work with the international community to improve cybersecurity of financial networks' (US Department of the Treasury, 2019).

While espionage is typically the primary objective, cryptocurrency heists are increasingly common (RecordedFuture, 2023). The Lazarus Group's attacks are strategically designed to generate revenue in order to circumvent the severe international sanctions imposed on North Korea (Siers, 2017; Park, 2021; Gulyás, 2022). The scale of the thefts – particularly from the decentralised finance (DeFi) sector – suggests the use of sophisticated, bespoke money laundering techniques to off-ramp stolen funds into fiat currency (i.e. government issued cash).

Cyber activities to illicitly obtain and launder virtual assets (cryptocurrency) are a key revenue stream for the regime, with over \$1.2 billion stolen since 2017.[2] Unlike traditional banking systems where assets can be frozen, cryptocurrencies operate on irreversible transactions and often with less security and Know Your Customer (KYC), Know Your Transaction (KYT) and Anti-Money Laundering (AML) controls.

The Lazarus Group employs a wide range of tactics to exploit the cryptocurrency ecosystem. These include large-scale exchange hacks, such as the \$280 million KuCoin breach in 2020, the \$624 million attack on Axie Infinity's Ronin Bridge and the \$100 million Harmony Bridge exploit in 2022. Beyond exchange breaches, the group conducts DeFi exploits by leveraging vulnerabilities in smart contracts to drain liquidity pools. They also deploy phishing and social engineering schemes, targeting employees of cryptocurrency firms with malware to gain access to internal systems and private keys.

Independent investigator ZachXBT attributes over \$200 million of laundered hack funds from over twenty-five cryptocurrency projects in hacks between 2020 and 2023 (ZachXBT, 2024) to the Lazarus Group. Other analytics firms estimate over \$3 billion USD in cryptocurrency tokens stolen since 2017 (ZachXBT, 2024).

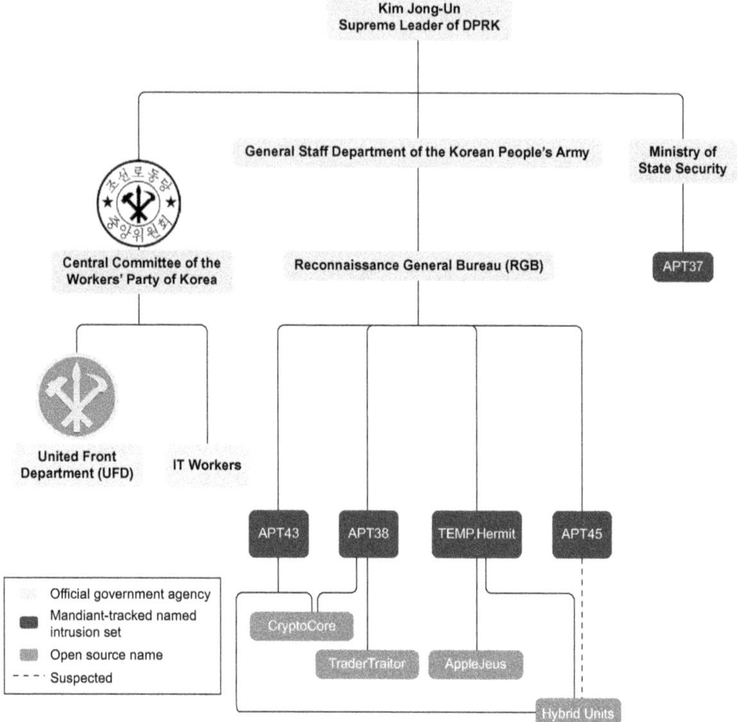

Figure 5.1 Assessed structure of DPRK cyber operations in 2024
(Long *et al.*, 2024)

Taylor Monahan (Security, Metamask and Incident Response, SEAL 911), a.k.a. 'Tayvano' on X, states:

> Crypto folks (hopefully) already know that Lazarus is one of the most prevalent threat actors targeting this industry. They rekt more people, companies, protocols than anyone else. But it's good to know exactly how they get in. Bc another smart contract audit won't save you...
>
> Instead of thinking you're invincible: Eliminate single points of failure Use hardware wallets / hardware MFA Don't run/build code from strangers Use diff devices for talking vs accessing crypto Don't judge Learn from other's mistakes Educate those around you STAY SKEPTICAL! (Tay, 2024c)

Tayvano's GitHub hosts years of resources, sorted into folders including 'hack and thefts', 'more hacks and thefts' and 'malicious shit' (Tayvano, 2025).

At the top of the collection of resources are the following quotes:

'If the Internet is like a gun, cyberattacks are like atomic bombs' – Kim Jon Il

'Cyberwarfare is an all-purpose sword that guarantees the North Korean People's Armed Forces ruthless striking capability, along with nuclear weapons and missiles' – Kim Jong-un

'The real purpose of the DPRK's cyber, military, policy, and political aggressiveness is ultimately to **control and subdue its own population and retain power**' – Tayvano

Her point? These are the bad guys, and regardless of cryptocurrency ideologies about autonomy from external political forces, immutability of digital infrastructure or censorship resistance, everyone needs to do what they can to avoid inadvertently funding authoritarian regimes to develop weapons of mass destruction.

The US FBI released a public service announcement in September 2024, declaring:

The Democratic People's Republic of Korea ('DPRK' aka North Korea) is conducting highly tailored, difficult-to-detect social engineering campaigns against employees of decentralized finance ('DeFi'), cryptocurrency, and similar businesses to deploy malware and steal company cryptocurrency.

North Korean social engineering schemes are complex and elaborate, often compromising victims with sophisticated technical acumen. Given the scale and persistence of this malicious activity, even those well versed in cybersecurity practices can be vulnerable to North Korea's determination to compromise networks connected to cryptocurrency assets. (IC3, 2024)

Attackers often have the time and resources to conduct extensive pre-operational research on their targets, enabling them to craft highly individualised false scenarios. For cryptocurrency targets, this includes fabricated job offers, investment opportunities or impersonations of recruitment agencies or trusted industry figures.

Although the FBI provides a range of technical recommendations to reduce the risk of such attacks, these remain socially engineered scenarios in which human error is ultimately inevitable.

North Korea's IT worker threat

In addition to elite hacking units, North Korea also deploys thousands of lesser skilled IT workers as a critical component of its cyber strategy. It is estimated that there are between three thousand and ten thousand IT workers deployed globally (Tay, 2024d). These individuals operate from call centres both in North Korea and abroad (i.e. Russia and China), with the goal of securing remote employment in global technology firms under false pretences. The cryptocurrency industry is being aggressively targeted, such as DeFi projects and exchanges, where it is normal for projects to hire remote, distributed teams, and even remain pseudonymous. The access provided creates a platform for espionage and disruption of business activities, and the targets can be high value. Revenue from illicit income and coordinated operations with state-sponsored hacking units contributes to funding North Korea's weapons of mass destruction and ballistic missile programmes, in direct violation of US and UN sanctions (IC3, 2023).

IT workers comb recruitment platforms like LinkedIn for remote work opportunities, aiming to secure work. Employment income is then funnelled to the North Korean government, which, in turn, provides the worker with a stipend to live on. Using fake identities, virtual private networks and engaging in legitimate work (such as software engineering), workers can then utilise insider access over time to steal proprietary information, introduce software backdoors, facilitate larger cyber operations and evade sanctions (US Department of Justice, 2023). In these operations, teams of five IT workers can manage over thirty fake identities in an effort to obtain and service software developer jobs (ZachXBT, 2025d).

As one SEAL posted in the chat:

> Yep. Investors, job candidates, partner project ceos, etc…
> Oh and lately a lot of forbes journalist doing an article on you (attacks getting more sophisticated).

These operations highlight North Korea's expansion into other areas of fraud, with the establishment of front companies that mimic legitimate IT support firms to also gain access and intelligence. For example, by copying large parts of legitimate company websites and offering services, North Korean actors aim to embed themselves in global IT supply chains to cause disruption and support the regime (RecordedFuture, 2025). These companies also post fake job ads, luring developers at established companies to download malware as part of job interview coding challenges and then compromising their devices. As hiring protocol checks evolve in the cryptocurrency industry, so do IT worker tactics.

An investigation by ZachXBT estimates that $2.76 million per month is being sent to North Korean IT workers in wages in 2025. 'To put this in perspective payments range from $3K–8K per month meaning they have infiltrated 345 jobs on the low end or 920 jobs on the high end', stated ZachXBT (2025e).

According to the SEAL chat, asking them to say 'Kim Jong sucks' is all it takes (as of October 2024, noting that the techniques of the IT workers are constantly evolving) to make them disconnect from a call when targeting you. Some companies are becoming more savvy to the infiltration attempts. In one story, a crypto exchange shows how the IT workers unravel when pressed on certain details of their identity or story by asking them about unscripted details, such as local restaurants (KrakenFX, 2025).

Another SEAL replied, 'they aren't trusted, they are sorta lowest rung of a long long ladder. Everything they do is monitored, as is everything their managers do, and their managers do'.

Jake Gallon, CEO of a Non-Fungible-Token (NFT) platform which allows people to move NFTs across blockchains, resorted to X to share an 'embarrassing' post about his personal experience with this type of infiltration. Access to his computer was gained during a Zoom interview in which he shared his screen to demonstrate his project, and over $100,000 in ETH and BTC assets were stolen. He explained:

> The person who interviewed me has a large social media presence, with some mutual followers, and I have ensured that all accounts links match up from our previous communications. Within 24 hours of the interview all of these exploits began to take place. (jake, 2025)

He proceeded to share: 'I'd like to talk with any security experts to help assess the situation'. In the thread of sympathy and condolences, there are multiple suggestions to contact @SEAL_Org, as well as a comment from Tayvano, suggesting: 'Yeah you have malware on your machine…Power down the device, use a different one to change passwords and be sure to log out your compromised device sessions so they can't use them. Please also get into SEAL and report the stolen funds so we can at least tag the addresses up', implying that an IT worker had won this round and the assets were long gone.

Even SEAL itself is not immune to this threat. 'Tanuki42', a SEAL contributor and investigator at Web3 security and incident response firm zeroShadow, reported: 'Meet Nick Franklin @0xNickLFranklin – Blockchain Security Engineer…or RGB operative hacking for DPRK? Seemingly this guy has had the entire industry fooled for years' (tanuki42, 2025), referring to an undercover DPRK operative that numerous SEALs had interacted with, who had tried to share malicious software with the co-founder of a large decentralised exchange. Another post that includes a screenshot of a conversation with an operative claims: 'So, it turns out that the Nick L Frankli account was run by DPRK, tied to the Radiant attack, and attempting to hack security researchers' (Daniel Von Fange, 2025). The account was linked to a cryptocurrency wallet that was in post-mortem reports of the $50 million Radiant hack in late 2024 to test sign the multisignature wallet.

Some SEALs in the chat reacted strongly. 'I remember thinking of inviting him here since he was doing so much public research [shocked sad face emoji]', stated one contributor, although there are further measures to prevent single authority additions to the group. 'Anyways feel foolish and paranoid now', another paranoid SEAL contributor, Infomorph, responded. 'This begs the question, how many DPRK operatives are already in here?', highlighting that not even SEAL, as a collective of security experts, is impervious to the threat posed by attackers.

pcaversaccio jumped in with an analysis of the trojan (a type of malware that hides within a legitimate file or program to gain access to your device) that the IT worker had tried to share with the co-founder and software engineer. The report stated: 'This incident, which is part of a broader deception and exploitation attempt, can be attributed with high confidence to the AppleJeus/Citrine Sleet/ UNC4736 DPRK team' (pcaversaccio, n.d.).

To counter such threats, it has been suggested that international cooperation, cybersecurity awareness and a comprehensive approach that addresses human and technical vulnerabilities are required (Perdana *et al.*, 2024). The US Department of Justice has announced coordinated actions against DPRK IT worker schemes, including an arrest, searches of 'laptop farms' and seizure of financial accounts and fraudulent websites (US Department of Justice, 2025, n.p).

SEAL Intel has launched an initiative to track and share intelligence on IT workers in order to help cryptocurrency companies identify potential operatives applying for remote roles. Individually, companies lack visibility into how malicious actors are connected and operate collectively. To address this, SEAL Intel's Information Sharing and Analysis Platform (ISAC) aggregates intelligence on fraudulent IT candidates across organisations, protecting blockchain firms from 'accidentally hiring a wolf in sheep's clothing' (Security Alliance, 2024).

Blockchain as a tool for sanctions evasion and financial laundering

Cryptocurrency is not just a target for hacks – blockchain technology has become a tool for laundering funds in state-sponsored financial crimes (particularly in the case of North Korea). The North Korean regime has systematically exploited vulnerabilities in decentralised networks to funnel stolen cryptocurrency into fiat currency, to redirect it back into state-controlled financial channels.

Using only publicly available information, ZachXBT and other DPRK tracers have analysed their techniques and behaviours, connecting hacks across multiple blockchains and cryptocurrency transaction mixers[3] to centralised exchanges, where funds can then be withdrawn via Over the Counter (OTC) trades (ZachXBT, 2024).

To obscure illicit transactions, North Korean actors employ privacy-enhancing protocols, such as the privacy transaction mixer to obfuscate the origin and movement of funds. Beyond on-chain privacy mechanisms, the regime leverages DeFi protocols, cross-chain bridges and OTC trading desks across Asia to bypass traditional financial controls such as KYC and AML and move illicit assets across blockchain ecosystems and into fiat currency. These tactics enable North Korea to evade international sanctions, convert stolen crypto into usable state funds and sustain its weapons programmes – all while exploiting and stealing from the very decentralised infrastructures designed to resist authoritarian control.

Policy, regulation and the future of decentralised security

The decentralised nature of blockchain systems makes it inherently difficult to fully control transactions or prevent illicit activity. Lawyers and policy advisors note that addressing financial crime in DeFi has proven particularly challenging for regulators (Rettig *et al.*, 2024). Some 'crypto-native' advisors recommend classifying genuinely decentralised DeFi protocols as critical infrastructure rather than financial institutions, arguing that this would both preserve their technological characteristics and allow for more effective, tailored regulation (Rettig *et al.*, 2024).

By contrast, the US government and its allies have taken a more punitive approach, criminalising privacy tools, sanctioning flagged cryptocurrency addresses linked to illicit activity and recommending that all cryptocurrency platforms and protocols implement counter-terrorist financing measures (including decentralised and centralised exchanges, bridges, instant swap services, mixers and privacy protocols). These include AML and KYC requirements (often in the form of centralised databases of customer details which are also targeted by hackers), as well as monitoring systems designed to detect possible DPRK-linked transactions. Law enforcement bodies, such as the FBI's Cyber Task Force, have also pursued cybercriminals directly.

Between 2013 and 2022, US federal agencies imposed more than $3.6 billion in fines on crypto market participants, underscoring that firms failing to deploy effective KYC, AML, trade surveillance and sanctions-screening programmes risk severe enforcement action (Solidus Labs, n.d.). While collaboration between law enforcement agencies and blockchain analytics firms has improved the tracing of illicit transactions, it has also raised concerns about privacy erosion and the weaponisation of financial oversight against users.

The US Treasury Department alleges that over $7 billion worth of virtual currency has been laundered through the decentralised 'mixer' protocol Tornado Cash[4] since its creation in 2019. This includes over $455 million stolen by Lazarus Group (US Department of the Treasury, 2022). The protocol was sanctioned in 2022 in line with Executive Order 13694 for having provided technological support for services in support of a cyber-enabled activity (US Department of the Treasury, 2022). The then Secretary of the Treasury for Terrorism and Financial Intelligence stated: 'Despite public assurances otherwise, Tornado Cash has repeatedly failed to impose effective controls designed to stop it from laundering funds for malicious cyber actors on a regular basis and without basic measures to address its risks' (US Department of the Treasury, 2022). This sanction was unprecedented, as it was the first time that the US government (via OFAC) sanctioned a software protocol and a Decentralised Autonomous Organisation (DAO),[5] rather than a traditional legal entity, individual or nation-state.

Amid the controversy, Tornado Cash developer Alexey Pertsev was arrested in the Netherlands on money laundering charges in August 2022, raising industry-wide concerns about the liability of developers for the uses of open-source code and the difficulties of enforcing retroactive compliance. In 2023, Coinbase funded a lawsuit challenging OFAC's actions, with plaintiffs arguing that decentralised protocols like Tornado Cash are essential for privacy and should not be subject to such sanctions.

pcaversaccio shared on X:

> I firmly believe that using Tornado Cash is a good thing to do for your on-chain financial privacy since the protocol has demonstrated its resilience, even after multiple attacks. NOT EVERYONE USING TC IS A BAD ACTOR but simply appreciates on-chain privacy! If you're looking to use an uncompromised interface, here are some secure IPFS hashes to consider. (pcaversaccio, 2024e)

Meanwhile, comments ensued in the SEAL chat ranging from, 'the principles of TC [Tornado Cash] were privacy-first and censorship-resistance and it works!', and 'Defi should be about freedom and anonymity', to 'privacy is completely doomed'. Herein lies the disparity between building with Cypherpunk principles of becoming uncensorable and ungovernable, and the reality of national security and consumer protection.

Another SEAL contributor, Michael Lewellen, resorted to the law to make their case, asserting:

> Today, I'm taking a stand against the Biden administration's unjust crackdown on crypto development. I've filed a lawsuit against the DOJ to challenge their flawed and unjust interpretation of the law… developers like me are facing baseless legal risks. The DOJ's broad interpretation of money transmission laws threatens the ability to build freely. (Michael Lewellen, 2025)

Although the sanctions against Tornado Cash were delisted in 2025 under the change of administration and a more pro-crypto industry policy stance (US Department of the Treasury, 2025), this incident marked a turning point in the governance of decentralised technologies, with far-reaching implications for blockchain security. The case re-surfaced debates about the accountability of decentralised infrastructure and the scope of government jurisdiction in regulating open-source code. The designation of Tornado Cash's smart contracts as sanctioned entities effectively blurred the line between code and personhood, suggesting that software itself can now be treated as an actor within global security frameworks. For blockchain security, this signified a shift in the risk landscape, where developers, DAOs and users of privacy-preserving tools may now be exposed to legal threats. The sanction also signals an emerging geopolitical consensus that privacy tools – especially those resistant to surveillance – constitute not just technical risks but national security concerns. As a result, the Tornado Cash precedent underscores the growing entanglement between privacy, decentralised security practices and state-based security practices.

A joint statement to the blockchain technology industry from the US, Japan and the Republic of Korea warns that the North Korean regime poses 'a significant threat to the integrity and stability of the international financial system' (US Department of State, 2025). The statement announces that 'The United States and Republic of Korea additionally attribute to the DPRK, based on detailed industry analysis, thefts last year against WazirX for $235 million and Radiant Capital for $50 million', as well as aggressive targeting with well-disguised social engineering attacks that deploy malware and compromise devices. The announcement points to SEAL as an example of 'newly established mechanisms to facilitate information sharing and incident response' (US Department of State, 2025).

Lazarus' activities highlight the geopolitics of blockchain security. While blockchain promises financial freedom, censorship resistance and decentralisation, it also possesses significant vulnerabilities that authoritarian states can exploit. The blockchain industry's response to these advanced security threats is fragmented, comprising anonymous independent investigators, protocol-level measures to slow or prevent money laundering (when implemented at all), volunteer white hat war rooms, centralised exchanges with the capacity to freeze funds and intervention by federal agencies.

UNsafe: the Radiant Capital hack

A post on X by Radiant Capital on October 18, 2024, read:

On October 16, 2024, Radiant Capital experienced a highly sophisticated security breach that resulted in the loss of $50 million USD. The attackers exploited multiple developers' hardware wallets through a highly advanced malware injection. The devices were compromised in such a way that the front-end of [@safe](https://x.com/safe) {Wallet} (f.k.a. Gnosis Safe) displayed legitimate transaction data while poisoned transactions were signed and executed in the background. This breach occurred during a routine multi-signature emissions adjustment process…To underscore the significance of this point, the compromise was completely undetectable during the manual review of the Gnosis Safe UI and Tenderly simulation stages of the routine transaction. This has been confirmed by external security teams, including [@_SEAL_Org](https://x.com/_SEAL_Org) and @HypernativeLabs. Radiant Capital has been working very closely with Seal911 and Hypernative and has since implemented stronger multisig controls. The U.S. law enforcement and @zeroshadow_io are fully informed of the breach and are actively working to freeze all stolen assets. The DAO is deeply devastated by this attack and will continue to work tirelessly with the respective agencies to identify the exploiter and recover the stolen funds as quickly as possible. (Radiant Capital, 2024a)

In an online article titled 'Radiant Capital Post-Mortem', the DAO elaborated:

> The attack compromised three Radiant developers, all of whom are long-standing, trusted contributors to the DAO. [...] The malicious actors exploited this normalcy, using the process to collect multiple compromised signatures over several attempts, all while mimicking the appearance of routine transaction failures. [...] The attackers subsequently drained approximately $50 million USD from the core markets on Arbitrum and BSC. Additionally, they exploited open approvals to withdraw funds from users' accounts. [...]
>
> The most concerning aspect of this attack is the high level of sophistication involved. The compromised devices presented no obvious warning signs beyond minor glitches and error messages during the signing process – issues commonly encountered when interacting with hardware wallets and Safe. These seemingly routine error messages were the only indicators of a deeper issue, which, under normal circumstances, would not have raised immediate concern. (Radiant Capital, 2024b)

Radiant was a hardware compromise as the attack vector to get a malicious transaction onto a hardware wallet (Radiant Capital, 2024). 'Basically, they intercepted the request from the software to the hardware wallet and swapped out the data that was to be signed', stated Robert MacWha, co-leader of the SEAL Whitehat Safe Harbor initiative. MacWha is referring to a process called 'blind signing' (Safe.eth, 2024). Instead of signing a transaction 'blindly', people can read the transaction information on the screen of the physical device and confirm by pressing buttons on the hardware wallet, rather than just viewing the details on their computer screen in the web application or browser.

Daniel Von Fange (DanielVF), SEAL Technical Council member and Senior Engineer at Origin Protocol, took to posting on X, stating:

> Yesterday's sophisticated 50 million Radiant Capital hack happened after attacker's trojaned the computers of multiple team members. Team members saw and verified good multisig data on screens, but their hardware wallets signed evil data. (Daniel Von Fange, 2024)

In other words, the hardware wallets actually signed a command to 'transferOwnership()' of a DeFi lending pool to the attackers. The post included a screenshot of the executed code highlighting which lines of code were the 'evil sigs' (signatures), with annotations that read '1. Take Ownership', '2. Change code' and '3. Steal Money' (Daniel Von Fange, 2024).

SEAL contributor and team member at major DeFi protocol banteg responded to the post: 'This level of attack is really scary. to my knowledge, the compromised signers have followed the best practices. they also used different combinations of os, software and hardware wallets, as well as simulated every transaction. where do we go from here? magical amulets?', emphasising the level of sophistication of modern attacks and the challenge to the industry to protect against them (banteg, 2024).

SEALs sprang into action in response to the event. Some developed improvements in the Safe Wallet user interface to improve the verifiability and safety of transactions (presuming the screen on the Ledger hardware device is reliable and not compromised) (Safe Global, n.d.).

Others contributed by analysing the attack. Tayvano pointed out in the SEAL chat that the Radiant hack techniques mirrored those of the $34 million Polynetwork hack in July 2023, arguing it was perpetrated by the same attacker.

One positive outcome of the Radiant attack is that it prompted developers and security professionals across Web3 to re-evaluate their defensive strategies. Following the hack, many teams adopted dedicated signing devices and reassessed the security of their multi-signature wallets and signing processes. Commenting in the SEAL chat, DanielVF noted the broader impact of SEAL's ability to provide clear, timely and accurate information during the incident: 'I think it's possible that the Radiant hack response by Seal 911 was an industry changing win – Might be the most behavior impact SEAL has ever had [...] We've seen multisig hacks before, and they did not result in people changing what they were doing'. The incident illustrates the dynamic and adversarial nature of blockchain security, in which each major exploit reshapes the strategies, expectations and infrastructures that underpin defensive efforts in decentralised systems.

The geopolitical implications of blockchain security

Blockchain security is increasingly entangled with geopolitical dynamics, as decentralised infrastructures intersect with state interests, national security priorities and global regulatory regimes. The capacity of blockchain systems to facilitate cross-border value transfer, resist surveillance and operate beyond traditional financial controls has attracted the attention of both state and non-state actors, including criminal networks and nation-state adversaries. As exemplified by the involvement of North Korea's Lazarus Group, along with the creation of US sanctions against Tornado Cash, blockchain security is not a purely technical concern but a site of geopolitical contestation.

Nation-states are increasingly treating vulnerabilities in blockchain protocols – and the privacy tools built on top of them – as issues of strategic importance, with implications for financial sovereignty, cyber defence and the future of internet governance. Securing decentralised networks, therefore, is not only a matter of protocol resilience but also of navigating shifting dynamics of international power and control. Within this landscape, decentralised communities, especially white hat hackers and initiatives like the Security Alliance, play a pivotal role in blockchain defence by mobilising collective intelligence and rapid-response capabilities beyond traditional institutional frameworks and across decentralised networks. Their distributed structures enable threat response, vulnerability disclosure and coordinated mitigation efforts that often complement, and at times outpace, state and corporate security apparatuses. Without these blockchain-native security efforts, the landscape for protocols and users would be far more precarious – reliant solely on fee-for-service security firms and hindered by slower processes for tracing and freezing stolen funds.

Conclusion

As blockchain technologies become increasingly embedded in global financial, technological and political systems, their security is emerging as a geopolitical concern. From criminal gangs and state-sponsored exploitation of decentralised financial protocols to the unprecedented sanctioning of software and DAOs, blockchain security now sits at the intersection of national security, international law and the decades-long contest over digital sovereignty. These developments challenge long-standing assumptions about the neutrality of technological infrastructure and the aspiration for autonomy within decentralised systems.

At the same time, large-scale responses to security threats are not confined to states and corporations. Decentralised technology communities, including white hat hackers, open-source investigators and collective security networks such as SEAL, are increasingly shaping the security landscape from within. Their efforts point to an emerging model of proactive, collective and distributed defence that reflects the ethos of decentralisation, sustaining the industry while reducing (but not avoiding) harm.

Ultimately, the geopolitical dimensions of blockchain security call for new frameworks of accountability, security and collaboration. As threats grow more sophisticated and the stakes increase, creatively navigating the tensions between openness, privacy, sovereignty and security will be critical to the future of decentralised technologies.

The chapter that follows details the play-by-play and insights from the largest hack in history.

Notes

1 The National Institute for Standards and Technologies (NIST) defines a cyberattack as 'Any kind of malicious activity that attempts to collect, disrupt, deny, degrade, or destroy information system resources or the information itself' (NIST, n.d.).

2 See UN report from March 7, 2023: 'Final Report of the Panel of Experts Submitted Pursuant to Resolution 2627 (2022)' (United Nations Security Council, 2023).

3 A mixer is a service that obfuscates transactions by pooling funds and then redistributing them to conceal a user's transaction graph.

4 Tornado Cash is a decentralised, non-custodial mixer built on the Ethereum blockchain. It allows users to obfuscate the source and destination of their cryptocurrency transactions by mixing them with

others in a smart contract 'pool', breaking the on-chain link between sender and recipient. Users deposit assets into the smart contract and then withdraw them using a cryptographic proof, ideally to a new address, making tracing much more difficult.

5 An automatically executing rule set according to pre-defined, algorithmically encoded rules on the blockchain that no central actor controls.

6

Bybit – The largest hack in history

By February 2025, with heightened public paranoia around all things digital and a personal update of my own operational security practices (please don't test them), I found myself more deeply embedded in the security mindset than when I first began this research. I had completed my PhD on resilience in decentralised technologies, spent over a year observing and participating in Security Alliance (SEAL) and collected a wealth of anecdotes and insights into how security is coordinated in decentralised contexts. My fieldwork for this book on digital security was nearly complete.

Through this journey, I had witnessed a clear evolution in how blockchain communities approach security – 'shifting left', as the saying goes, by embedding security practices earlier in the software development lifecycle in response to addressing insecurity and ever-evolving attack vectors.

And then it happened: the largest hack in history.

This chapter tells the story of that event, drawing on insider perspectives from within the security community. It traces black hats, white hats and many shades of grey in action, revealing how incident response is coordinated across the ecosystem, when it succeeds in protecting the interests of end-users, and when it fails due to selfish ambition. The chapter underscores the enduring reality that insecurity is a permanent condition. It also reveals the emergent infrastructure, norms, controls and feedback loops that scaffold how decentralised communities collectively respond to insecurity.

Rekt: the Bybit exchange attack

'People keep calling this is [sic] the "largest crypto hack ever" but I think it might be the largest hack ever…period?' (Tay, 2025b), mused Tayvano on Twitter, proceeding to refer to a swathe of previous attacks, including Ronin Bridge, $620 million (2022, the Democratic People's Republic of Korea [DPRK]), Polynetwork, $611 million (2020, not DPRK) and Coincheck (2018, not DPRK) (Tay, 2025c).

Suspicious outflows from Bybit exchange of $1.46 billion were first reported on February 21, 2025, by white hat ZachXBT in his Telegram channel 'Investigations by ZachXBT'. Bybit is among the largest cryptocurrency exchanges globally, based in Dubai, and sporting around $4 billion of 24-hour trading volume. ZachXBT, crypto-famous for his cat-and-mouse tracing of North Korean hacker activity, later confirmed that the attackers were indeed the Lazarus Group by linking the stolen funds to a wallet address previously used in a DPRK-attributed hack (ZachXBT, 2025b). His reward for solving the $1.5B mystery was a bounty of around $31,000 USD from a crypto trading intelligence platform, awarded in its native token (Arkham, 2025).

The Bybit CEO, Ben Zhou, confirmed the hack and reported it to law enforcement authorities (Bybit, 2025a). The race then began to trace and blacklist attacker addresses as the FBI released a public service announcement for RPC node operators, exchanges, cross-chain bridges and Decentralised Finance (DeFi) services to block transactions (IC3, 2025), as Lazarus Group follows a pattern of trading funds into ETH, swapping ETH for BTC and offloading Bitcoin via exchanges and over the counter (OTC) desks across Asia.

Meanwhile, in the SEAL chat, on February 22, 2025 (the day of the hack), someone asked,

'What's happening with bybit?'.

pcaversaccio responded in the same minute: 'we're on it'.

The comments start coming in as people realise what's happening: 'oof', 'oh damn'.

One SEAL asked: '@pcaversaccio do you have any indicators where the compromise was. Most specifically if the Safe webapp might be affected?' (Which indeed turned out to be the root cause of the exploit, according to forensics released days after the event.)

pcaversaccio replied 'sorry guys can't tal[k,] later$'.

Inside the exploit

While the full forensic reconstruction of the hack would take days, security researchers were already piecing together the likely attack vector in the immediate aftermath. Intense discussions ensued across chats, forums and incident channels as the community worked to understand what had happened. Discussions in the SEAL chat highlighted the nature of the hack and noted its resemblance to previous tactics, including DMM Bitcoin ($305 million USD in cryptocurrency tokens in May 2024), WazirX ($230 million in July, 2023) and Radiant Capital hack ($50 million in October) (Tay, 2024a), as well as less serious 'lols' about the fact that the CEO of Bybit had launched a livestream to announce that everything was under control.

The hack was a blind signing issue, similar to the Radiant Capital hack, but this time through a compromise of a wallet user interface to insert the malicious transaction. Unlike smart contract exploits that traditionally plagued DeFi protocols, the origin of this 'kill chain' was a phishing attack against a developer who worked at SAFE (the multi-signature wallet company) to compromise their device with malware disguised as fake trading software. The attacker was then able to infiltrate the developer's AWS (Amazon Web Services) cloud computing environment and covertly insert a malicious front-end by directly modifying the front-end S3 bucket to specifically target Bybit when interacted with.

The attackers then withdrew cryptocurrency from the Bybit exchange, which led to Bybit accessing a cold storage wallet to deposit more funds into the exchange. Three cold storage signers from Bybit, including the CEO, authorised the transaction on Safe's front-end to transfer 30,000 ETH, but without checking the transaction on a local device; they instead were signing a malicious transaction to upgrade the cold storage vault, ready to be drained. Then, the malicious front-end was removed from Safe to cover the hackers' tracks, and the heist began, draining the entire ETH cold storage vault of $1.5 billion (a very large amount to store in one wallet).[1] Within hours, the breach was the subject of live Twitter Spaces, Discord discussions and Telegram alerts.

According to Safe's website, their wallet is used by 'Vitalik Buterin and leading web3 projects to secure over $100 billion'. The fake front-end wasn't detected, meaning that the vulnerability could have been used to target *any* wallet that interacted with Safe. The attackers attempted to cover their tracks by removing the front-end after the hack, likely in the hope of reusing the same attack vector in future. Measures have already been made to make this more challenging (for example, hosting cryptographically hashed canonical links to the website on decentralised storage platforms, and writing software scripts to improve signing verifications).

'Lazarus is good. Lazarus is crazy good' reflected Tarun Chitra, CEO and Founder of Gauntlet, while talking about the event on a well-known crypto podcast (Unchained, 2025: at 9.02). 'They are trying to compromise every project in crypto', replied the co-host (Unchained, 2025: at 22.46). This was certainly not the first time DPRK had stolen funds by exploiting an organisation's multisignature wallet rather than compromising private keys directly, as was the case with the Radiant Capital and WazirX hacks (Tayv, 2024). In crypto security, old tactics die hard, and the hackers will keep on using them as long as they are effective.

Crisis response in a decentralised context

As blockchain explorers updated in real time, thousands of onlookers – some concerned, some opportunistic – began tracing the flow of funds (ZachXBT, 2025a). Laundering the funds has been an incredibly coordinated effort by hundreds, if not thousands of coordinated individuals across blockchain infrastructures (ZachXBT, 2025b).

For some time, security community contributors have been sharing flow charts of how crypto money is moved and making public appeals to slow down the laundering of funds. In a 2023 post on X, Tayvano (security white hat and 'DPRK chaser' from Metamask) urged people and platforms to take more responsibility for tracing and slowing down DPRK's actions:

> The blockchain is a **public** ledger. It is transparent for all to see. **You** can follow the money. You can watch them co-mingle funds stolen in separate hacks & re-use addresses. You can do this all w/ info that is shared publicly with the hopes that you **will** follow the money. (Tay, 2023)

She continued in another post on X:

> 150,000+ ETH 7k+ addresses 10k+ transactions And that's my last count. I had to take a nap. I'm really tired and behind. Everyone else. Please fucking slow their asses down. Don't *let* them get a billion fucking dollars out *easily*. (Tay, 2025d)

The post linked to a Public Service Announcement by the FBI calling '**RPC node operators**, exchanges, bridges, blockchain analytics firms, DeFi services, and other virtual asset service providers to block transactions with or derived from addresses TraderTraitor actors [TraderTraitor being a US Federal Agency name for the specific Lazarus malware and group] are using to launder the stolen assets' (IC3, 2025).

Not all actors in the ecosystem were cooperative in slowing down DPRK-linked money laundering. While some cross-chain bridge services responded by disabling front-ends and blocking blacklisted wallet addresses, they lacked the ability to fully shut down the underlying protocols (Chainflip Labs, 2025). Other crypto platforms, however, effectively bought time for DPRK operatives to process funds by reframing the issue as an ideological debate about censorship and decentralisation, rather than taking immediate practical action. These actors questioned who has the authority to judge good and bad behaviour within permissionless systems, even when the entity in question is the DPRK whose operations are known to fund a nuclear weapons programme, while continuing to benefit handsomely from the transaction volume and associated fees generated by the laundering process.

SEAL 911 contributors and others publicly called out the complicity of the crypto platforms that facilitated the money laundering, benefiting from over $5 million in fees (BlockTracker, 2025). Tayvano shared on X:

> In 10 days flat, DPRK has bridged all ~500,000 ETH (~$1.3 billion USD) stolen from Bybit to Bitcoin. Kim Jong Un sends his deepest gratitude to @THORChain, @asgardex, and @exchcx. Without their faux-cypherpunk grandstanding + blatant lies, this would have never been possible. (Tay, 2025e)

Another commentator on X put it this way:

> THORChain just helped North Korea launder $605 million. No KYC, no off switch, no resistance. Lazarus Group jacked Bybit for $1.5 billion in February 2025, then funneled the stolen ETH through THORChain like it was built for them. Over five days, $2.91 billion in volume ripped through, $860 million in a single day, while THORChain pocketed $3 million in fees. That's not innovation – that's negligence at best, greed at worst…Now? THORChain's reputation is torched. FBI's on them, institutions are walking, and they're the poster child for DeFi's worst-case scenario. They could have stopped this. They didn't. Not by accident – by choice. (Yogi, 2025)

According to reports from Bybit, $42.89 million in funds (or approximately 3 per cent) was frozen (Bybit, 2025b), $2,178,797 USDT was paid out by Bybit to eleven different hunters in bounties (Zhou, 2025a), and the rest was successfully laundered.

By March 6, 2025, pcaversaccio stated: 'It has taken 19 days (not counting prior preparation) to pull off the biggest CEX [centralised exchange] hack in history so far. It all started with an innocent looking Docker project' (pcaversaccio, 2025a). Below the message, pcaversaccio shared a screenshot of the timeline of events and key findings to date from the forensic investigation report of the compromised wallet company (Zhou, 2025b).

A well-known crypto podcast reflected on the event in an episode titled, 'How the $1.5 Billion Bybit Hack Could Have Been Prevented'. During the episode, Mudit Gupta, SEAL contributor and Chief Information Security Officer at Polygon Labs said, 'there is no other industry like this', referring to the inconceivability of such a significant amount of funds being stored in one wallet and then compromised (Shin, 2025a).

On another episode of the same podcast, senior investigator Jonty from zeroShadow Web3 security and incident response firm shared that 'you have to be paranoid when you make these transactions', referring to multi-signature signing procedures (Shin, 2025b). Jonty went on to explain that hacking cryptocurrency is the easiest way for North Korea to steal funds and convert it to cash, highlighting that the crypto industry needs to see this as a problem and become more serious about its security posture. 'We are certainly losing the cat and mouse game', they stated (Shin, 2025b).

Beyond the blockchain

Meanwhile, SEALs were annoyed in the chat. With reputation gains bolstered by an ethos of 'credit where credit is due' as a crucial reward for contributions to ecosystem security, Bybit released a statement that didn't credit SEAL for their support in coordinating the war room. For Bybit, the unfolding situation was not just a catastrophe but a test of crisis coordination and communications in decentralised finance.

Posting on X, they stated:

> It's been a challenging 24 hours, but one thing is clear – our partners have our backs. The support from @AntalphaGlobal, @bitgetglobal, @MEXC_Official, @galaxyhq, @falconxnetwork, @LidoFinance, @fenbushi, @pionex_com and many others has been nothing short of incredible. Your trust, quick action, and solidarity mean everything. We're moving forward, stronger and more determined than ever. Thank you for standing with us. (Bybit, 2025a)

The post linked to a press statement sharing a 'heartfelt thanks to the global cryptocurrency community for the overwhelming support' as they united against security threats (Bybit, 2025c).

Instead of talking about the mechanics or scale of the incident, people pointed out that SEAL was not mentioned. AndrewMohawk took to X to rant: 'cant believe they didn't include @_SEAL_Org who have been running a warroom, providing advice, co-ordinating and doing work since minutes after it happened'. A reply to Bybit X from Crypto Lord also pointed out: 'Lol no mention of @zachxbt support ? Bybit deserves to be liquidated' (Crypto Lord, 2025).

While others tried to minimise the significance of Bybit's oversight by pointing out that the post would have come from a public relations team, not security folk, SEAL contributors got it amended by asking nicely and privately through back channels.

On the technical side, pcaversaccio didn't skip a beat after supporting the war room – immediately jumping into solver mode to build open-source code. On March 6, he shared a software code script to add warning for untrusted delegate calls and help prevent Safe signing errors in future (pcaversaccio, 2025b).

The implications of the hack are devastating to the reputation and legitimacy of the cryptocurrency industry more broadly. AndrewMohawk marked the incident as 'a tragedy and a huge loss of confidence in the web3 ecosystem's security' (AndrewMohawk, 2025).

In other words, 'it should be possible to make mistakes, and not die', as stated by DanielVF from Origin Protocol (Daniel Von Fange, 2025).

AndrewMohawk went on to urge an ecosystem-wide approach to security, stating, 'We should be striving together to implement controls that mean everyone is safer and not rely on individual implementations of security features' (McPherson, 2025).

The hack was a win for users. ByBit had enough liquidity to pay back the loans to users who wanted to withdraw funds from the exchange, with the CEO assuring 'we can cover the loss', thanks to the company's large size and revenue (Zhou, 2025c). In other words, unlike previous, high-profile centralised exchange hacks where the exchange declared bankruptcy and the users were left with nothing,[2] this hack wasn't an entire loss for users. In fact, those who hadn't seen the news wouldn't know any differently.

Yet, the industry-wide response from blockchain protocols was disappointing – fragmented by ideological divisions and inconsistent actions in the wake of the hack. Heated debates arose over whether transactions should be halted, or whether it violated Cypherpunk principles to restrict anyone's access to blockchains, even in the case of DPRK-affiliated wallets. Meanwhile, some actors strategically benefited from the indecision, profiting from transaction fees while the stolen funds were effectively laundered (Godbole, 2025).

High-profile incidents involving international consumer protection failures and links to DPRK activity inevitably drew the attention of regulators. In response, proponents of decentralised protocols warned that fragmentation and self-interest within the industry undermine its long-term viability. They emphasised that the repeated illicit use of decentralised infrastructure would absolutely provoke drastic regulatory action, threatening the very principles the ecosystem seeks to uphold. 'Governments will likely escalate measures if they perceive decentralized protocols as systemic risks. This could include sanctioning protocol addresses, pressuring infrastructure providers, blacklisting entire networks or going after the builders', stated Rachel Lin, CEO of SynFutures (Yun, 2025).

The Bybit hack and its aftermath highlight the strengths, nuances and challenges of blockchain security in action. Culture, ideology, reputation, incentives and the geopolitical entanglements shape how threats are perceived and responded to in decentralised security. This case reinforces that blockchain security is not merely about cryptographic robustness or smart contract audits, but also about the human and institutional relationships and arrangements that define how insecurity is addressed in decentralised systems.

Conclusion: rethinking digital security

Numerous projects, protocols and security service providers used the incident as a marketing opportunity to create content about how their services or solutions 'could have prevented the Bybit hack' and 'how to keep your crypto safe' to avoid the next $1.5 billion hack (which will come, given the run of success by Lazarus against the industry so far) (Blockaid, 2025; Maz, 2025). Yet, the reality of digital security is that insecurity will always be with us, so we may as well coordinate in relation to it. As stated by AndrewMohawk, 'security incidents WILL happen, everyone makes mistakes' (MacPherson, 2025).

These types of events, as depicted throughout this book, reframe digital security not as a fixed state to be achieved, but as a continuous process. This process involves negotiating vulnerability and insecurity to make insecurity visible, enabling collaboration and coordination to address insecurities both pre-emptively and reactively as they arise.

The Bybit hack demonstrates how the resilience of digital infrastructure in the years to come will not be determined by the elimination of risk, but by the ability of systems and communities to anticipate, adapt to and recover from it. The case serves as a stark reminder that decentralised security – and digital security more broadly – operates within a persistent state of insecurity. In this view, insecurity is not a failure of digital systems but the foundational reality from which security must be built. The incident exemplifies how insecurity is a structural condition of digital life – one that must be navigated through the ecosystem-wide alignment of incentives and the infrastructure and norms to coordinate action.

As digital infrastructures are increasingly the substrate on which everyday interactions occur, securing them requires collaboration across technical, legal, economic and institutional domains. It is in this interplay between the social and the technical that security is negotiated, made and remade. To understand and improve digital security, we must pay close attention to how people organise, coordinate and respond to a persistent state of insecurity. Thus, security is a practice embedded in the everyday maintenance of systems that remain, by their very nature, insecure.

The chapter that follows synthesises the key tensions and insights explored in this book, reflecting on the core provocations of this book about the future of computer security and drawing out the critical lessons from decentralised technology communities for digital security more broadly.

Notes

1 Order of events based on the hack report PDFs, originally hosted at https://docsend.com/view/s/rmdi832mpt8u93s7# (accessed February 27, 2025, now deleted) but available in Tayvano, 2025a; and Safe, 2025.
2 See Hajdarbegovic, 2014.

Part IV

Securing digital futures

Epilogue – Living with insecurity

Introduction

The central question of this book has not only been how security is enacted within decentralised technology communities, but also what these practices reveal about the broader condition of digital security. At its core, this inquiry confronts a deeper problem of how we live with insecurity in an increasingly digital world. Through ethnographic analysis, the preceding chapters have shown that decentralised systems make visible dynamics that are not unique to blockchain, but increasingly define digital infrastructures at large: persistent insecurity, fragmented responsibility and accountability, the challenge of aligning incentives and emergent modes of security governance. These dynamics complicate dominant cybersecurity paradigms that rely on centralised control, hierarchical accountability and compliance-based enforcement, leaving users with little recourse in the event of cybersecurity incidents.

This epilogue returns to the guiding question, 'what can decentralised technology communities teach us about digital security?', and argues that while decentralised security practices do not offer a ready-made solution, they provide a powerful lens for reimagining how we organise, incentivise and govern security in a world where insecurity is the norm rather than the exception. This lens reveals repeatable patterns that underpin decentralised responses to insecurity: (i) the infrastructure and actors that render insecurity legible and make action possible, (ii) norms that guide who gets to act, under what conditions and on whose behalf, (iii) controls that anchor best-practice responses and coordination mechanisms, and

(iv) feedback loops that translate lessons learned into updated tools, expectations and community standards.

Fittingly, this chapter is presented as an epilogue – not to provide final solutions, but to embrace an open, reflective and forward-looking stance. Just as decentralised systems resist closure, our understanding of digital security must remain adaptive and oriented towards continuous negotiation. In this sense, decentralised technology communities illuminate not only novel security practices, but collective ways of living with insecurity.

One night in Bangkok

As I entered the palatial lobby, smooth jazz music floated through the foyer as people in suit jackets and silk dresses lined the stools of the bustling bar.

I knew the Security Alliance (SEAL) event was being held at the Presidential suite, hosted by a 'crypto-rich' benefactor (i.e. someone who had made significant wealth in the cryptocurrency industry). Their generosity in hosting a social event for volunteer contributors was motivated by the rationale that SEAL was 'securing their bags'.

My problem was that the lifts required an access card to reach the desired level. I was determined not to message in the group chat like a noob ('newbie') being stuck in the foyer and waiting for a white hat rescue. Without hesitating, I moved through the muted atmosphere of the dimly lit lobby and calmly stepped into the first elevator doors that opened like I knew how to get to where I was going.

The elevator went up with other passengers gradually exiting. Level 2…Level 12…Level 29…close enough. I gave a polite smile and brushed past the remaining passengers to step out of the lift. Now I had to find a way down four floors and a way into the Presidential suite…

The words of SEAL 911 lead, pcaversaccio, echoed in my head: 'the security mindset' (ethnographic interview). There was no air conditioning in the stairwell to take the edge off the humidity of Bangkok. As I traversed down five flights in the thirty-degree heat, I maintained my thesis that the security door would open from the inside (a lesson garnered from a previous experience of getting stuck in a broken-down lift in Thailand). I held my breath slightly as I reached for the door handle of Level 24 and pressed, hoping I wouldn't have to spiral down twenty-four more flights of stairs and set off a fire alarm to get out. It opened. Around the hallway corner, the door to the suite was already cracked open. I was in.

When I opened the group chat, others had encountered the same issue.

'You need a key card to access the floor. Now I'm just riding the elevator. 911!'

'I'm at floor 5 with the same issue'.

'Asked the front desk and they let me up'.

'As you walk in the building turn left and give them your name and they will escort you'.

'Haha', I responded. 'I rode to floor 29 and took the fire stairs down'.

Matta (co-founder of The Red Guild and lead of the SEAL frameworks initiative) responded: 'Hacking right there!'.

'Respect', replied Daniel VF (security contributor at Origin Protocol).

Hacking my way into this gathering was one thing. Not getting hacked while attending a high-profile crypto event overseas was quite another. News came out that week that multiple scams were circulating during the DeFi Security Summit (DSS) and Ethereum Developer Conference (DevCON) when thousands of crypto-folks were in town.

> There is a scam going around where someone is creating fake luma [event platform] events that impersonate real ones, then they send out a realistic email saying 'hurry the event is full, you need to mint this NFT to be guaranteed access' and of course the link is a drainer. I know of someone who got drained (thankfully only $10). (Jeffrey Scholz, 2024)

I had played a series of interactive quizzes built by SEAL contributors and The Red Guild called 'The Phishing Dojo', and failed miserably (The Red Guild, n.d.). The game features mock scenarios of notorious phishing and scam threats in the crypto space, including fake conference organiser emails, event invitations and DMs (direct messages) from investors. The player is asked to identify whether each scenario was phishing or not, and was incredibly difficult.

Word also spread regarding SMS blaster attacks to mobile phones along Bangkok's BTS Skytrain line to phish cryptocurrency holders during DevCon. An SMS blaster attack works by using a device that mimics a cellular base station, allowing scammers to send fraudulent text messages to nearby mobile phones without being blocked by network filters. These messages often trick recipients into revealing personal information or clicking on malicious links. The gang responsible sent close to one million malicious SMS text messages over the three-day period of the conference before reportedly being arrested (Whittaker, 2024).

Sadly, attacks around the city were not limited to phishing attempts and data raking. News came out halfway through the crypto conference of an event on the island of Phuket: 'Ukrainian robbed of 8m baht in digital money in Phuket…ropes and tape were left at a crime scene' (Chuenniran, 2024). The sickening reality of the physical threat that comes with being associated with an industry known for one-way financial transactions was palpable in the chat as the news was shared.

> The victim initially talked to the men on the balcony of the room. Later he needed to go to a toilet. When he opened the toilet room, two men were waiting for him there…
>
> The two men, with faces covered, tied his limbs with ropes and cable ties. The victim said that Mr Arman told him to transfer USDT (Tether) 500,000; otherwise, they would break his fingers. Mr Arman held a hammer and the man who covered his face had a long knife.
>
> Mr Leibov said he asked the gang to halve the ransom. After he made the transfer, worth about 8.56 million baht, the gang tied him to a bed, warned him to not report the crime, collected their belongings and left the scene. (Chuenniran, 2024)

Two Ukrainians, an Armenian and a Russian – reportedly in their late teens and early twenties – were later arrested and charged with armed robbery in connection with the heist (Nation Thailand, 2024). Incidents such as these underscore the persistent and pervasive nature of insecurity – both physical and digital.

Lessons for digital security – persistent insecurity

A central finding of this book is that decentralised communities do not offer a blueprint for security as a fixed or universal condition; rather, they reveal the insecurity of digital interactions.

Centralised systems are vulnerable to specific types of failure, including single points of failure and incentive structures that are often misaligned with the interests of end-users. When your bank is scammed, it writes off the loss and returns the funds to you. When your data is hacked, you receive an email apology and perhaps an invitation to a class action lawsuit that never goes anywhere, or some bonus loyalty points.

In contrast, the precarity revealed in decentralised systems is a condition of participation. In these ecosystems, attack surfaces are distributed across loosely connected components, the technical infrastructure is in a constant state of development and individuals bear significant responsibility for their own conduct online. As a result, stakeholders must work to make insecurity legible in order to navigate environments where security guarantees are weak, roles are often informal and accountability is distributed among developers, users, security auditors, founders, white hats and governance participants. Thus, decentralised infrastructure does not eliminate insecurity – it foregrounds it.

Decentralised technology communities make visible what is often obscured in traditional digital systems: that security is not externally provisioned for users. In decentralised systems, insecurity is not hidden – it is rendered visible and unavoidable as a condition to be governed. There is no illusion of a secure perimeter, no central authority to assign blame and no corporate abstraction to absorb risk. Instead, insecurity is distributed, experienced and acknowledged as part of everyday life. It is, in other words, persistent – not because decentralised systems are uniquely flawed, but because all digital infrastructure is inherently vulnerable. The difference is that decentralised systems refuse to conceal this reality.

Without centralised authorities to enforce rules or patch vulnerabilities, decentralised communities must govern insecurity through distributed cooperation. This underscores a broader truth: all digital security relies not only on technical guarantees, but also on human behaviour, economic incentives, legal provisions and governance structures – tools and norms that surface insecurity and coordinate who can act in response. This recognition lays the groundwork for a different approach to digital security. Whereas centralised systems often treat insecurity as an exception – an anomaly to be patched – decentralised systems treat it as a baseline condition and design accordingly. Persistent insecurity becomes the driver of a security mindset shaped by paranoia, continuous maintenance and adaptive governance. It animates the very ethos of decentralisation: the practice of building and owning one's own infrastructure (Nabben, 2023c). In this context, communities must continuously construct and reconstruct their capacity to adapt and respond to threats and crises.

To decentralise security, then, is not to deny the reality of insecurity – but to confront it, live with it and find ways to navigate it. This is reflected in the blockchain industry through the emergence of new actors – such as the blockchain white hat hacker – and through unlikely collaborations between stakeholders, such as federal agencies and pseudonymous blockchain sleuths. It is also evident in new institutional arrangements, such as SEAL as a donation-backed, not-for-profit initiative supported by venture capitalists, major protocol foundations, Decentralised Autonomous Organisations (DAOs) and private donors. Innovations in incentives (both economic and reputational) and legal mechanisms (such as Safe Harbor provisions) further demonstrate the creative governance experiments emerging in response to this persistent insecurity.

Persistent insecurity, then, is not the end of the story – it is the terrain on which the work of decentralised security begins.

Fragmented responsibility and accountability

So, as pointed out to me by colleagues upon reading this manuscript in draft form, why would anyone want to expose themselves to the precarious nature of decentralised systems and rely on decentralised security? The answer is not that decentralised security is easier or more foolproof. Rather, those who build and operate within these systems do so because it aligns with a broader set of values and visions underpinning decentralised infrastructure: a commitment to open-source software, privacy and autonomy.

The understanding of digital security as a practice – and indeed, a mindset of vigilance, paranoia and a way of being – can be traced to the cultural lineage of hacker communities, independent cryptographers, and the Cypherpunk movement (as shown in Chapter 2). For these groups, security was never something to be outsourced to institutions or guaranteed from above, but something to be actively cultivated through individual competence, collective experimentation and constant iteration.

The goal then, for these communities, is not to retreat to centralisation, but to evolve the sociotechnical systems and infrastructure that make decentralised security a viable alternative.[1] In practice, this is no small task. Security remains one of the biggest hurdles to the adoption of blockchain technologies and the most pressing concern for their legitimacy.

Decentralised systems demonstrate that it is possible to coordinate meaningful security responses across distributed actors without centralised command structures. Yet, security outcomes often remain centralised in key ways. Even when security is organised through decentralised means, trust tends to reconsolidate around competent and credible actors. Protocols typically rely on a handful of core security team members and multisignature (multisig) wallet signers; exploits are patched by a small band of renowned white hat volunteers; and protocol communities often defer to a few respected audit firms for expert reviews.

Infrastructure, norms, controls, feedback

Moments of crisis reveal the informal but highly responsive networks that underpin decentralised security. As seen in high-profile incidents such as the Bybit exploit (Chapter 6), security coordination often involves a complex choreography between independent researchers, blockchain analytics firms, white hat hackers and protocol teams – mobilising rapidly to trace stolen funds, alert exchanges, freeze assets and pressure protocols to suspend or censor wallet addresses.

Security, then, emerges as one of the core domains in which decentralised systems must actively build social, technical, legal and economic infrastructure in order to survive. It is, in this sense, a fundamentally sociotechnical process – one where code and incentives are necessary but insufficient.[2]

What sustains decentralised security is not merely the presence of bug bounties or audit contracts, but the cultivation of shared norms around responsibility and conduct that cultivate community alignment. This evolution is evident in the shift from an ecosystem dominated by rent-seeking service providers to options driven by reputation-fuelled, volunteer-based collaborative security networks. Controls shape how stakeholders respond in moments of crisis – such as through mechanisms like the white hat Safe Harbor agreement, which defines the boundaries of legitimate intervention. Routine practices like wargame red-teaming exercises and incident post-mortems serve as feedback mechanisms, folding lessons learned back into tools, protocols and community expectations. The value lies not in any single artefact or actor, but in the way artefacts, stakeholders and norms co-produce visibility, authority and permission to act.

In such settings, stakeholder engagement and incentive alignment become essential to enable sustained cooperation in mitigating cascading failures across a deeply interconnected ecosystem. These settings surface new types of actors.

Blockchain white hat hackers as protagonists

If decentralised security depends on making insecurity legible, then white hat hackers are among its primary instruments of legibility. Their presence offers a kind of implicit promise: when protocols or users cannot secure themselves, someone will step in to help. Yet this promise is never guaranteed – it is continually renegotiated through shifting moral norms, sustainability challenges, incentive structures (or lack thereof), prioritisation and boundary-setting within the community. Rather than framing white hats as either heroic saviours or contradictory figures, this analysis understands their controversies as the governance of insecurity in motion.

The broader lesson for digital security is not to replicate the white hat model wholesale, but to adopt a sensitivity to the fact that security categories are performed through situated practice, and their legitimacy depends on how communities render interventions against insecurity visible, credible and sustainable. SEAL's activities reflect efforts to build the tools and infrastructure (a.k.a. boundary objects) necessary to provision and sustain white hat services, while also engaging with and enhancing industry-wide security capabilities. The generalisable lesson is that 'good actor' identities are not fixed traits but levers by which to create and reinforce constructive security behaviours. Systems can be designed and culture-propagated to reinforce constructive behaviour as visible, valuable and supported over time.

The need for incentive alignment

Decentralised systems are experiments in *cryptoeconomic* coordination – relying on incentives like staking slashing conditions or security bug bounties to drive secure behaviour (Nabben, 2023a). While these mechanisms can be powerful, they also expose the limits of relying solely on economic incentives rooted in assumptions of rational, self-interested actors. Without alignment with social, moral and institutional frameworks, economic incentives alone are insufficient to ensure security.

Beyond the growing industry of professional security providers, decentralised ecosystems depend on a dispersed network of actors – private firms, independent researchers, pseudonymous volunteers – and a patchwork of incentives, including reputation, bug bounty platforms and retroactive donations. Yet no consistent or sustainable framework exists to support this critical work. Many security contributors operate without stable funding or institutional backing, overwhelmed by escalating threats and unpaid requests for assistance. This lack of sustainable incentives hinders efforts to encourage grey hats towards responsible disclosure and limits the appeal of white hat behaviour, even when large bounties are offered. For example, as mentioned in Chapter 3, the hacker of Euler Finance ignored a \$1 million bug bounty in favour of exploiting the vulnerability for greater personal gain.[3]

Security bounties themselves are often inconsistently funded or poorly scoped, leaving major gaps in coverage and reliability. The resulting ecosystem depends heavily on informal labour and goodwill – conditions that are unsustainable and vulnerable to burnout, fragmentation and legal risk.

Effective decentralised security requires more than monetary incentives: it depends on effective tools, shared values and trusted processes. SEAL, and broader communities within Ethereum and Web3, have developed a culture of security rooted in Cypherpunk ideals, reputational norms and mutual obligation. In systems where formal enforcement is limited to what is encoded in software (i.e. 'code is law' [Lessig, 1999], in its narrow, blockchain-native sense), informal norms are as important as effective infrastructure. These norms shape behaviour not through coercion or profit alone, but through belonging, recognition, and responsibility.

In decentralised ecosystems, where no single actor is fully in charge, everyone becomes partially responsible. Within this reality, infrastructure maintenance becomes a foundational – yet often overlooked – component of digital security. As Vinsel and Russell (2020) observe, society tends to valorise innovation while undervaluing the everyday labour of keeping systems running. This dynamic is acute in blockchain ecosystems, where resources and attention flow to new projects while existing protocols rely on underfunded maintainers – developers, auditors, node operators, white hats and volunteer investigators – whose unglamorous work keeps systems secure or reveals their flaws. By foregrounding maintenance as a central concern to security, this book reframes decentralised security not as a heroic battle against threats but as a mundane, necessary, collective and ongoing practice of responsibility.

Security for users

The experience of holding and transacting cryptocurrency for the user is still not without many flaws. Despite advances in protocol-level protections (such as smart contract audits), users continue to face substantial risks, often due to poor usability, limited technical literacy and inadequate safeguards against human error. Loss of private keys, phishing attacks and malicious smart contract approvals are common ways in which users lose access to their assets – frequently with no recourse or recovery mechanisms.

In this context, users become security actors, not just end beneficiaries. The emphasis on user self-sovereignty, while central to the ethos of decentralisation, places a significant burden on individuals to manage their own security in high-stakes environments, or to defer back to centralised third parties to maintain custodianship of assets on their behalf. The reality of digital infrastructures being insecure by default brings users into sharper focus as active participants in the security landscape. Unlike traditional systems where security is often abstracted away from end-users, decentralised technologies distribute both risk and responsibility throughout the ecosystem. This redistribution compels users – not just developers or auditors – to remain vigilant, informed and engaged in practices that contribute to collective security. As DanielVF puts it, 'It should be possible to make mistakes, and not die' (Daniel Von Fange, 2025). When responsibility is diffused, it also must be internalised in the mindset and practices of every user.

Computer security as the future of law?

Mark Miller's vision of 'computer security as the future of law' (2017) articulated over two decades ago reminds us that security is the foundation upon which all digital interactions depend. Miller positioned security mechanisms as the digital equivalent of legal enforcement, arguing that in an increasingly computerised world, security would function as a form of governance that would replace traditional legal institutions with automated rule enforcement (Miller, 2017). His ideas resonated with the early ideologies of decentralised technology communities – where cryptographic guarantees, smart contracts and decentralised governance mechanisms were expected to provide security and trust between unknown parties without reliance on legal intermediaries.

Miller's thesis of security as 'the future of law' (2017) offers a prescient frame for understanding the stakes of decentralised digital infrastructure security. In systems where formal legal enforcement is limited or absent, code 'becomes' law (i.e. the primary medium through which rules are expressed and enforced). Code provides enforceable constraints (i.e. time locks, withdrawal limits, multi-signature permissions) that seem law-like because they enable and constrain actions. Yet, this vision of 'law encoded' cannot be realised unless the infrastructure itself is secure.

Ethnographically, those constraints only function as legitimate 'law' when insecurity has first been rendered visible, measurable and accountable to the people who must act. In practice, this means that the infrastructure of security (i.e. Safe Harbor white hat engagement agreements, security playbooks, best practice frameworks, intelligence, war rooms, post-mortems and so on) becomes the procedural substrate that decides when coded powers may be exercised and by whom. The blockchain ledger functions as the record of who does what, but who is invited and how 'good faith' contributions occur are primarily social.

Before decentralised systems can meaningfully afford users the ability to secure themselves, they must first improve the resilience of their own architecture. Far from eliminating the need for law, the blockchain space has instead shown that digital security itself must be governed, and that governance involves human coordination and facilitation. Vulnerabilities at the protocol and inter-protocol level, as well as the state of the security industry, local and global threats, lack of sustainable incentives and the burden of responsibility on the user, undermine the very possibility of secure coordination, governance and enforcement.

The ethnographic implication of this is clear: computer security becomes 'law' not by replacing institutions with code, but by coupling enforceable controls to accountable procedures for seeing, deciding and intervening under persistent insecurity. Law, here, is the infrastructure and patterned practices that turn insecurity into a governable event, record the crisis responses and return projects to ordinary functioning. Thus, instead of the ideological blockchain 'code as law' aspiration coming alive in the encoded rules of a protocol, the governance of blockchain security is less an atrophied pre-agreed rule set than situated guidance for action among distributed stakeholders that is assembled through infrastructure and norms that make insecurity legible enough to act.

Computer security and white hats

Viewed through Miller's 'computer security as the future of law', white hats occupy the procedural hinge between code-based rules and their legitimate function. If measures such as war rooms, Safe Harbor agreements, multi-signature wallets, time locks and protocol freezes are the *instruments of* security legibility infrastructure, white hats help decide *when* and *how* those instruments are exercised through both technical prowess and convening the actors who hold decision rights. In effect, they perform quasi-legal or policing roles – detective, first responder, sometimes moral judge – inside micro-jurisdictions constituted by keys, code and contracts (as in the case of publicly calling out mixing protocols for not freezing despite known money laundering uses). Their authority is not granted once and for all; reputation is earned incident by incident through visible competence and ongoing contribution.

That authority is also contested. White hats draw boundaries against adjacent figures (for example, salaried responders, bounty hunters and opportunistic 'rescuers') through ethical practices that sort rescue from ransom. A key differentiator here is operating according to the white hat code of ethical conduct, especially regarding not prioritising financial self-gain ahead of users' interests (for example, responsibly disclosing a vulnerability that is discovered, rather than publicly exploiting it and then negotiating a fee to return the funds).

As a stakeholder class, then, white hats are best understood as a distributed layer that translates diffuse insecurity into governable actions. Their emergence is the concrete way 'future-of-law' claims live in the wild – not by replacing institutions with code, but by coupling code's enforceability to auditable procedures for seeing, deciding and intervening. The broader implication for digital security is not to elevate the 'white hat' label as a moral ideal, but to design infrastructure – technical, social and economic (in the way that blockchain communities are) – that makes such intervention legible, pre-authorised, time-bounded and accountable.

Conclusion

Insecurity characterises the landscape of decentralised systems. Before decentralised infrastructures can provide security to people, the security of the infrastructure itself must first be addressed, or at least accounted for. It is clear that security is not merely a technical issue to be solved in code; it is the foundation for the legitimacy and functionality of digital interactions. Security is also a precondition for effective decentralised organising – and, more broadly, for online life.

In this persistent state of insecurity, the question remains as to whether these systems can ever reliably be protected for people to count on. Yet, initiatives such as SEAL show that it is not software code alone that is relied on to address insecurity. Blockchain white hats, tools and shared initiatives crystallise an emergent security legibility infrastructure. They are neither classic in-house security staff nor anonymous bug bounty hunters. Instead, they operate as trans-organisational first responders whose trusted standing rests on their capacity to render insecurity visible enough for collective action, between white hats and blockchain project security personnel, as well as across protocols, government agencies and legislators. This is then reinforced via cultural norms and behaviours.

Decentralised security communities provide an alternative framework – one where *insecurity* is distributed across participants and protocols and incentivised through economic, legal and reputational mechanisms. This approach invites a fundamental rethinking of how security is built and maintained in digital infrastructure. They demonstrate that, in the absence of centralised authority, security can still emerge through voluntary cooperation, moral commitments and distributed expertise. It also requires a shift in the security mindset from reactive patching to proactive threat anticipation, and from institutional oversight to community-driven, ecosystem-wide strategies, predicated on sharing information and learnings from every incident. Yet, these arrangements are also experimental and contested, depending on a small number of expert actors, volunteer labour, donor funding and mutual, reputation-based responsiveness across the industry to trace, pause and patch incidents in times of crisis.

At the heart of this analysis is a recognition that security cannot be outsourced to a single entity – be it a government agency, a corporation or an algorithm. Instead, security is distributed, adversarial and deeply embedded in the ways digital systems are designed, governed and maintained. This is not a call for decentralisation as an ideological end goal, but rather an acknowledgment that insecurity is addressed through cooperation, via infrastructure, norms, controls and feedback. The blockchain ecosystem demonstrates how open networks can self-organise security practices, not despite their decentralised nature but because of it – an insight that is increasingly relevant as global digital infrastructure becomes more interconnected and interdependent.

The Bybit attack, and many others like it, is a stark reminder: in decentralised systems, security is never guaranteed. Instead, the story of decentralised digital security is not one of conclusion but of continuation – a 'to be continued' experiment in how we might improve security in an insecure world.

Notes

1 For example, see the Ethereum Foundation's 'Trillion Dollar Security Initiative': Ethereum Foundation (2025), 'Announcing the Trillion Dollar Security Initiative', May 14. Available online: https://blog .ethereum.org/2025/05/14/trillion-dollar-security.

2 As Bijker and Law (1994) argue, technologies are co-constituted through networks of human actors, institutions, practices and material artefacts. Security is no exception.

3 See also the Cetus Protocol DeFi hack of 2025 on the Sui blockchain protocol, in which a $6 million bounty was offered in exchange for returning approximately $56 million in stolen funds. In an on-chain message, Cetus stated: 'In exchange, you can keep 2,324 ETH (~$6M) as a bounty, and we will consider the matter closed and will not pursue any further legal, intelligence, or public action'; see: Sei Vision (2025) 'Message from Cetus'. Available online: https://suivision.xyz/ object/0x5d373ba22cf02764df82f5495030730 79b7e04b956a06c4cf 0b7d3987f6ba192

References

Abbate, J. (1999). *Inventing the Internet*. MIT Press.

Abbate, J. (2010). 'Privatizing the Internet: Competing Visions and Chaotic Events, 1987–1995'. *IEEE Annals of the History of Computing*, 32 (1): 10–22. https://doi.org/10.1109/MAHC.2010.24

Abrams, Z. (2023). 'He Stole $200 Million. He Gave it Back. Now, the Hacker is Explaining Why'. *Coinage Media*, June 30. https://www.coinage.media/s2/he-stole-200-million-he-gave-it-back-now-hes-ready-to-explain-why (accessed November 13, 2025).

Abrams, Z. (2024). 'Prisma Finance Hacker Defends Exploit, Demands Public Apology'. *The Block*, March 30. https://www.theblock.co/post/285776/prisma-finance-hacker-defends-exploit-demands-public-apology (accessed November 13, 2025).

Anderson, R. (2001). 'Why Information Security is Hard – An Economic Perspective'. *17th Annual Computer Security Applications Conference* (ACSAC '01), IEEE Computer Society, December, 358–65. https://doi.org/10.1109/ACSAC.2001.991552

Andrew Mohawk (@AndrewMohawk) (2025). 'The Bybit hack is a tragedy…' X, February 28. https://x.com/AndrewMohawk/status/1895297455048270063 (accessed November 13, 2025).

Arkham (@arkham) (2025). 'BREAKING: BYBIT $1 BILLION HACK BOUNTY SOLVED…' X, February 21. https://x.com/arkham/status/1893033424224411885 (accessed November 13, 2025).

Assange, J. (2012). *Cypherpunk: Freedom and the Future of the Internet*. OR Books.

Baker, K. (2025). 'What Is an Advanced Persistent Threat (APT)?', *CrowdStrike*, March 4. https://www.crowdstrike.com/en-us/cybersecurity-101/threat-intelligence/advanced-persistent-threat-apt/ (accessed November 13, 2025).

Banteg (@banteg) (2024). 'This level of attack is really scary…' X, October 18. https://x.com/bantg/status/1847120310618767633 (accessed November 13, 2025).

Bamford, J. (1983). *The Puzzle Palace: A Report on America's Most Secret Agency*. Penguin.

Baran, P. (1964). *On Distributed Communications: I. Introduction to Distributed Communications Networks*. RAND Corporation eBooks.

Bay, M. (2019). 'Conversation With a Pioneer: Larry Roberts on How He Led the Design and Construction of the ARPANET'. *Internet Histories* 3 (1): 68–80. https://doi.org/10.1080/24701475.2018.1544727

Be'ery, T. (2021). 'The BadgerDAO Hack: What Really Happened and Why It Matters'. *Zengo*, December 15. https://zengo.com/the-badgerdao -hack-what-really-happened-and-why-it-matters (accessed November 13, 2025).

Ben Zhou (@benbybit) (2025a). '3.4.25 Executive Summary on Hacked Funds…' X, March 4. https://x.com/benbybit/status/1896798476945 744010 (accessed November 13, 2025).

Ben Zhou (@benbybit) (2025b). 'Bybit Hack Forensics Report…' X, February 26. https://x.com/benbybit/status/18947687360848885929 (accessed November 13, 2025).

Ben Zhou (@benbybit) (2025c). 'Bybit is Solvent even if this hack loss is not recovered…' X, February 21. https://x.com/benbybit/ status/1892969284587966869 (accessed November 13, 2025).

Berg, C., S. Davidson and J. Potts (2019). 'Blockchain Technology as Economic Infrastructure: Revisiting the Electronic Markets Hypothesis'. *Frontiers in Blockchain* 2 (22). https://doi.org/10.3389/fbloc.2019.0 0022

Bijker, W. E. and J. Law (eds) (1994). *Shaping Technology/Building Society: Studies in Sociotechnical Change*. MIT Press.

Birch, K., D. Cochrane and C. Ward (2021). 'Data as Asset? The Measurement, Governance, and Valuation of Digital Personal Data by Big Tech'. *Big Data & Society* 8 (1). https://doi.org/10.1177/2053 951721101730 8

Blockaid (2025). 'How to Prevent the Next $1.5B Bybit Hack: A Strategic Approach to Solving Blind Signing'. *Blockaid*, February 21. https:// blockaid.io/blog/how-to-prevent-the-next-15b-bybit-hack-a-strategic -approach-to-solving-blind-signing (accessed November 13, 2025).

Blockchain Security Series (2024). 'Blockchain Security Series 14 – Fredrik Svantes (Security Research Lead @ Ethereum Foundation)'. Video, posted October 2. YouTube, 1:17:16. https://www.youtube.com/watch ?v=RVl5Bvyxs9U (accessed November 13, 2025).

BlockTracker (@block_tracker21) (2025). 'In February, @THORChain processed $6B+ in swap volume…' X, March 3. https://x.com/block_tracker21/status/1896566998601232696 (accessed November 13, 2025).

Bodó, B. and A. Giannopoulou (2020). 'The Logics of Technology Decentralization – The Case of Distributed Ledger Technologies'. In *Blockchain and Web 3.0: Social, Economic, and Technological Challenges*, edited by M. Ragnedda and G. Destefanis, 114–29. Routledge.

Bodó, B., J. K. Brekke and J.-H. Hoepman (2021). 'Decentralisation in the Blockchain Space'. *Internet Policy Review* 10 (2): 1–12. https://doi.org/10.14763/2021.2.1560

Bowker, G. C., K. Baker, F. Miller and D. Ribes (2009). 'Toward Information Infrastructure Studies: Ways of Knowing in a Networked Environment'. In *International Handbook of Internet Research*, edited by J. Hunsinger, L. Klastrup and M. Allen, 97–117. Springer.

Buterin, V. (2014). 'Ethereum: A Next-Generation Smart Contract and Decentralized Application Platform'. https://ethereum.org/content/whitepaper/whitepaper-pdf/Ethereum_Whitepaper_-_Buterin_2014.pdf (accessed April 1, 2025).

Buterin, V. (2012). 'Bitcoin Adoption Opportunity: Teenagers'. *Bitcoin Magazine*, February 28. https://bitcoinmagazine.com/culture/bitcoin-adoption-opportunity-teenager-1330407280 (accessed November 13, 2025).

Buterin, V. (2017). 'The Meaning of Decentralization'. *Medium*, February 6. https://medium.com/@VitalikButerin/the-meaning-of-decentralization-a0c92b76a274 (accessed November 13, 2025).

Buterin, V. (2023). 'Make Ethereum Cypherpunk Again'. *Vitalik.eth*, December 28. https://vitalik.eth.limo/general/2023/12/28/cypherpunk.html (accessed November 13, 2025).

Bybit (@Bybit_Official) (2025a). 'We have reported the case to the appropriate authorities…' X, February 21. https://x.com/Bybit_Official/status/1893044807217393910 (accessed November 13, 2025).

Bybit (@Bybit_Official) (2025b). 'A coordinated effort led to the freezing of $42.89M…' X, February 23. https://x.com/Bybit_Official/status/1893687749229563958 (accessed November 13, 2025).

Bybit Press (2025c). *Bybit*. https://www.bybit.com/ed-ED/press/post

Calvão, F. (2018). 'Crypto-Miners: Digital Labor and the Power of Blockchain Technology'. *Economic Anthropology* 6 (1): 123–34. https://doi.org/10.1002/sea2.12136

Carse, J. (1986). *Finite and Infinite Games*, 1st edn. Free Press.

Cavez-Dreyfuss, G. and T. Wilson (2021). '"White Hat" Hacker Returns Most of $600 Mln Crypto Tokens Taken – Poly Network'. *Reuters*, August 13. https://www.reuters.com/technology/white-hat-hacker-has-returned-nearly-all-600-million-crypto-tokens-taken-tuesday-2021-08-12/ (accessed April 30, 2025).

CertiK (2024). 'Vanity Addresses and Address Poisoning'. https://www.certik.com/resources/blog/vanity-address-and-address-poisoning (accessed September 3, 2025).

Chainflip Labs (@Chainflip) (2025). 'We're aware of the hacker's attempts...' X, February 22. https://x.com/Chainflip/status/1893222347252875386 (accessed November 13, 2024).

Chawla, V. (2023). 'BlockSec Prevents $5 Million from Being Stolen on Paraspace'. *The Block*, March 17. https://www.theblock.co/post/220761/blocksec-prevents-5-million-from-being-stolen-on-paraspace (accessed November 13, 2025).

Chuenniran, A. (2024). 'Ukrainian Robbed of B8m in Digital Money in Phuket'. *Bangkok Post*, November 10. https://www.bangkokpost.com/thailand/general/2899637/ukrainian-robbed-of-b8m-in-digital-money-in-phuket (accessed November 13, 2025).

CISA (2022). 'TraderTraitor: North Korean State-Sponsored APT Targets Blockchain Companies'. April 20. https://www.cisa.gov/news-events/cybersecurity-advisories/aa22-108a (accessed November 13, 2025).

CISA (n.d.). 'North Korea Cyber Threat Overview and Advisories'. https://www.cisa.gov/topics/cyber-threats-and-advisories/advanced-persistent-threats/north-korea (accessed March 17, 2025).

Coleman, E. G. and A. Golub (2008). 'Hacker Practice: Moral Genres and the Cultural Articulation of Liberalism'. *Anthropological Theory* 8 (3): 255–77. https://doi.org/10.1177/1463499608093814

Coleman, G. (2012). *Coding Freedom*. Princeton University Press.

Collier, J. (2018). 'Cyber Security Assemblages: A Framework for Understanding the Dynamic and Contested Nature of Security Provision'. *Politics and Governance* 6 (2): 13–21. https://doi.org/10.17645/pag.v6i2.1324

Cos (@evilcos) (2024). 'After checking, this friend's wallet was really "hacked" by AI...' (translated from Chinese by Grok), X, November 22. https://x.com/evilcos/status/1859752658061623593 (accessed November 13, 2025).

Crypto Lord (@Thecryptolord_) (2025). '@Bybit_Official @Antalpha Global...' X, February 22. https://x.com/Thecryptolord_/status/1893307925818445953 (accessed November 13, 2025).

Cryptoanarchy.wiki (1992–98). https://cypherpunks.venona.com/raw/ (accessed April 1, 2025).

Daniel Von Fange (@danielvf) (2024). 'Yesterday's sophisticated 50 million Radiant Capital hack…' X, October 17. https://x.com/danielvf/status/1847023591117795708 (accessed November 13, 2025).

Daniel Von Fange (@danielvf) (2025). '@pcaversaccio It should be possible to make mistakes…' X, February 27. https://x.com/danielvf/status/1895099332317139327 (accessed November 13, 2025).

Davis, J. L. (2020). *How Artifacts Afford: The Power and Politics of Everyday Things*. MIT Press.

Davis, J. L. and J. B. Chouinard (2016). 'Theorizing Affordances: From Request to Refuse'. *Bulletin of Science, Technology & Society* 36 (4): 241–48. https://doi.org/10.1177/0270467617714944

De Filippi, P. and B. Loveluck (2016). 'The Invisible Politics of Bitcoin: Governance Crisis of a Decentralised Infrastructure'. *Internet Policy Review* 5 (3). https://doi.org/10.14763/2016.3.427

De Filippi, P., M. Mannan and W. Reijers (2020). 'Blockchain as a Confidence Machine: The Problem of Trust & Challenges of Governance'. *Technology in Society* 62: 101284. https://doi.org/10.1016/j.techsoc.2020.101284 (accessed November 13, 2025).

DeFi Security Summit (2024a). 'DSS 2024 – November 8 – Day 1'. Video, posted November 8, YouTube, 9:54:02. https://www.youtube.com/watch?app=desktop&v=gMg6Smve-i0 (accessed November 13, 2025).

DeFi Security Summit (2024b). 'Panel | What Your Auditor REALLY Thinks…' Video, posted November 8, YouTube, 9:54:02. https://www.youtube.com/watch?v=gMg6Smve-i0 (accessed November 13, 2025).

DeFi Security Summit (2024c). 'The State of DeFi Security – DSS 2024 Edition | Day 1'. Video, posted November 8, YouTube, 9:54:02. https://www.youtube.com/watch?v=gMg6Smve-i0 (accessed November 13, 2025).

DeFi Security Summit (2025). 'The 2016 Shanghai Attacks: History and Technical Deep Dive | Hudson Jameson'. Video, posted January 22, YouTube, 24:30. https://www.youtube.com/watch?v=hYPCtij_h4o (accessed November 13, 2025).

DeNardis, L. (2014). *The Global War for Internet Governance*. Yale University Press.

Diffie, W. and M. E. Hellman (1976). 'New Directions in Cryptography'. *IEEE Transactions on Information Theory* 22 (6): 644–54. https://doi.org/10.1109/TIT.1976.1055638

Dolomite (@Dolomite_io) (2024). 'We have reached a deal with the whitehat…' X, March 24. https://x.com/Dolomite_io/status/1771922337912291607 (accessed November 13, 2025).

Drexler, E. K. (1991). 'Hypertext Publishing and the Evolution of Knowledge'. *Social Intelligence* 1 (2): 87–120.

Dunn Cavelty, M. and A. Wenger (2020). 'Cyber Security Meets Security Politics: Complex Technology, Fragmented Politics, and Networked Science'. *Contemporary Security Policy* 41 (1): 5–32. https://doi.org/10.1080/13523260.2019.1678855

DuPont, Q. (2017). 'Experiments in Algorithmic Governance: A History and Ethnography of "The DAO", a Failed Decentralized Autonomous Organization'. In *Bitcoin and Beyond*, edited by M. Campbell-Verduyn, 157–77. Routledge.

DuPont, Q. and B. Fidler (2016). 'Edge Cryptography and the Codevelopment of Computer Networks and Cybersecurity'. *IEEE Annals of the History of Computing* 38 (4): 55–73. https://doi.org/10.1109/MAHC.2016.49

Edelman, G. (2021). 'The Father of Web3 Wants You to Trust Less'. *Wired*. November 29. https://www.wired.com/story/web3-gavin-wood-interview/ (accessed November 11, 2025).

Electronic Frontier Foundation (2014). 'The Crypto Wars: Governments Working to Undermine Encryption'. January 2. https://www.eff.org/document/crypto-wars-governments-working-undermine-encryption (accessed November 13, 2025).

Era.zksync.network (n.d.). 'SEAL 911: Multisig'. *zkSync Era Block Explorer*. https://era.zksync.network/address/0x265d1C1B10E644014D461b65a2e5414D3686cF22 (accessed April 2, 2025).

Ethereum Foundation (2018). 'A Conversation with Stewart Brand (Devcon4)'. Video, posted December 11, YouTube, 50:34. https://www.youtube.com/watch?v=oLGZdLpHl1w (accessed November 13, 2025).

Etherscan (2024). 'Input Data Messages (IDM) | Etherscan. Ethereum (ETH) Blockchain Explorer'. https://etherscan.io/idm (accessed November 13, 2025).

Faustino, A. (2023). 'Web3 and the Entrepreneurial Imaginary of the 2022 Lisbon Web Summit'. *Anthropology Today* 39 (4): 24–27. https://doi.org/10.1111/1467-8322.12830

Flock (6'3) (@melgibsonfan99) (2025). 'ZachXBT spent years conning brainlets…' X, January 21. https://x.com/melgibsonfan99/status/1881655915482685695 (accessed November 13, 2025).

Foobar (@0xfoobar) (2025). '> scammer makes zachxbt memecoin…' X, January 21. https://x.com/0xfoobar/status/1881662061031432211 (accessed November 13, 2025).

Foresight Institute (2022). 'Shielded Transactions. Bitcoin's Privacy Problem (with Zooko Wilcox)'. Video, posted September 3, YouTube, 1:05:36. https://www.youtube.com/watch?app=desktop&v=WXXVoK92zN8&feature=youtu.be (accessed November 13, 2025).

FS-ISAC (n.d.). Financial Services Information Sharing and Analysis Center. https://www.fsisac.com (Accessed December 1, 2024)

Gieryn, Thomas F. (1983). 'Boundary-Work and the Demarcation of Science from Non-Science: Strains and Interests in Professional Ideologies of Scientists'. *American Sociological Review* 48 (6): 781–95.

Gilbert, F. (1971). 'Intellectual History: Its Aims and Methods'. *Daedalus* 100 (1): 80–97.

Gilmore, J. (1999). 'Please Title This Page. (Page 2)'. *Cryptome.org*, April 17. https://cryptome.org/jya/cp-who.htm (accessed November 13, 2025).

Godbole, O. (2025). 'THORChain Sees Record $4.6B Volume After Bybit's $1.4B Hack'. *CoinDesk*, March 4. https://www.coindesk.com/markets /2025/03/04/thorchain-sees-record-usd4-6b-volume-after-bybit-s-usd1 -4b-hack (accessed November 13, 2025).

Gulyás, A. (2022). '"Lazarus" The North Korean Hacker Group'. *Proceedings International Scientific Conference STRATEGIES XXI: The Complex and Dynamic Nature of the Security Environment*, February 8. 75–83. https://doi.org/10.53477/2668-6511-22-08

Hajdarbegovic, N. (2014). 'Mt. Gox Statement Claims It Made Conscious Decision to Halt Transactions'. *CoinDesk*, updated April 10. https:// www.coindesk.com/markets/2014/02/25/mt-gox-statement-claims-it -made-conscious-decision-to-halt-transactions (accessed November 13, 2025).

Hassan, S. and P. De Filippi (2017). 'The Expansion of Algorithmic Governance: From Code Is Law to Law Is Code'. *Field Actions Science Reports: The Journal of Field Actions*, 17 (December): 88–90. https:// journals.openedition.org/factsreports/4518 (accessed November 13, 2025).

Hayes, A. (2019). 'The Socio-Technological Lives of Bitcoin'. *Theory, Culture & Society* 36 (4): 49–72. https://doi.org/10.1177/0263276419826218

Hine, C. (2000). *Virtual Ethnography*. SAGE Publications Ltd.

Howe, C., J. Lockrem, H. Appel, E. Hackett, D. Boyer, R. Hall, M. Schneider-Mayerson, A. Pope, A. Gupta, E. Rodwell and A. Ballestero (2016). 'Paradoxical Infrastructures: Ruins, Retrofit, and Risk'. *Science, Technology, & Human Values* 41 (3): 547–65. https://doi.org/10.1177 /0162243915620017

Hoyng, R. (2023). 'From Bitcoin to Farm Bank: An Idiotic Inquiry into Blockchain Speculation'. *Convergence* 29 (4): 1015–32. https://doi.org /10.1177/13548565231154104

Hughes, E. (1997). 'A Cypherpunk's Manifesto'. In *The Electronic Privacy Papers*, edited by B. Schneier and D. Banisar, 285–87. John Wiley & Sons, Inc.

Hunt, J. (2023). 'KyberSwap Hacker Demands Full Control in Bizarre On-Chain Message'. *The Block*, November 30. https://www.theblock.co/post/265429/kyber-hacker-control-message (accessed November 13, 2025).

Hwang, S. (2023). 'Digital Frontlines: The Emerging Role of Cryptocurrencies in Hybrid Warfare & Geopolitics'. University of Pennsylvania ScholarlyCommons, April 30. https://repository.upenn.edu/entities/publication/156c4e2c-ae94-4497-98fb-fec7ce5c0c3d (accessed November 13, 2025).

IC3 (Internet Crime Complaint Center) (2024). 'North Korea Aggressively Targeting Crypto Industry'. *IC3, Federal Bureau of Investigation*, September 3. https://www.ic3.gov/PSA/2024/PSA240903 (accessed November 13, 2025).

IC3 (Internet Crime Complaint Center) (2025). 'North Korea Responsible for $1.5 Billion Bybit Hack'. *IC3, Federal Bureau of Investigation*, February 26. https://www.ic3.gov/PSA/2025/PSA250226 (accessed November 13, 2025).

IC3 (Internet Crime Complaint Center) (2023). 'Cryptocurrency Fraud Report'. *IC3, Federal Bureau of Investigation*. https://www.ic3.gov/AnnualReport/Reports/2023_IC3CryptocurrencyReport.pdf (accessed November 13, 2025).

IFTF Staff (2010). 'IFTF Mourns Paul Baran'. *Institute for the Future*, September 1. https://www.iftf.org/future-now/article-detail/iftf-mourns-paul-baran/ (accessed November 13, 2025).

Immunefi (2022). 'The True Origin of Hacks & Top Web3 Vulnerabilities'. https://immunefi.com/research (accessed November 13, 2025).

Immunefi (2023). 'The Rekt Test'. https://immunefi.com/blog/expert-insights/rekt-test/ (accessed November 19, 2025).

Immunefi (2024). '2024 Annual Report'. https://immunefi.com/research (accessed March 3, 2025)

Insikt Group (2023). 'North Korea's Cyber Strategy'. *RecordedFuture*, June 23. https://www.recordedfuture.com/research/north-koreas-cyber-strategy (accessed November 13, 2025).

Insikt Group (2025). 'North Korea's Fraudulent IT Employment Scheme'. *RecordedFuture*, February 13. https://www.recordedfuture.com/research/inside-the-scam-north-koreas-it-worker-threat (accessed November 13, 2025).

itsjustcornbro (@itsjustcornbro) (2024). 'web2 fixes this'. X, July 14. https://x.com/itsjustcornbro/status/1812460291604545919

jake (@jakegallen_) (2025). 'The past 24 hours I've been battling...' X, April 10. https://x.com/jakegallen_/status/1910437715671474512 (accessed November 13, 2025).

Jarvis, C. (2020). *Crypto Wars: The Fight for Privacy in the Digital Age: A Political History of Digital Encryption*. CRC Press.

Jarvis, C. (2021). 'Cypherpunk Ideology: Objectives, Profiles, and Influences (1992–1998)'. *Internet Histories* 6 (6): 1–27. https://doi.org/10.1080/24701475.2021.1935547

Jaspers, J. D. (2017). 'Managing Cartels: How Cartel Participants Create Stability in the Absence of law'. *European Journal on Criminal Policy and Research* 23: 319–335. https://doi.org/10.1007/s10610-016-9329-7

Jeffrey Scholz (@Jeyffre) (2024). 'There is a scam going around…' X, November 10. https://x.com/Jeyffre/status/1855652717081088375 (accessed November 13, 2025).

Jewett, T. and R. Kling (1991). 'The Dynamics of Computerization in a Social Science Research Team: A Case Study of Infrastructure, Strategies, and Skills'. *Social Science Computer Review* 9 (2): 246–75. https://doi.org/10.1177/089443939100900205

Kow, Y. M. and C. Lustig (2018). 'Imaginaries and Crystallisation Processes in Bitcoin Infrastructuring'. *Computer Supported Cooperative Work (CSCW)* 27 (2): 209–32. https://doi.org/10.1007/s10606-017-9300-2

KrakenFX (2025) 'How We Identified a North Korean Hacker Who Tried to Get a Job at Kraken'. *Kraken*. May 1. https://blog.kraken.com/news/how-we-identified-a-north-korean-hacker (accessed November 13, 2025).

Lamport, L., R. Shostak and M. Pease (1982). 'The Byzantine Generals Problem'. *ACM Transactions on Programming Languages and Systems* 4 (3): 382–401. https://doi.org/10.1145/357172.357176

Landau, S. (2000). 'Standing the Test of Time: The Data Encryption Standard'. *Notices of the AMS* 47 (3): 341–49.

Lavoie, D. (1990). 'Prefatory Note: The Origins of "The Agorics Project"'. *Market Process*, 8 (2).

Lavoie, D., H. Baetjer and W. Tulloh (1990). 'High Tech Hayekians: Some Possible Research Topics in the Economics of Computation'. *Market Process* 8 (spring): 120–46.

Ledger (n.d.). https://www.ledger.com/

Le Monde (2025). 'Seven Held in France for Kidnapping and Torture of Crypto Figure'. January 25. https://www.lemonde.fr/en/pixels/article/2025/01/25/seven-arrested-in-france-for-kidnapping-and-torture-of-crypto-co-founder_6737412_13.html (accessed November 13, 2025).

Lessig, L. (1999). *Code: And Other Laws of Cyberspace*. Basic Books.

Levy, S. (1984). *Hackers: Heroes of the Computer Revolution*. Delta.

Levy, S. (2002). *Crypto: How the Code Rebels Beat the Government Saving Privacy in the Digital Age*. Penguin Books.

Levy, S. (2010). *Hackers: Heroes of the Computer Revolution – 25th Anniversary Edition*, 25th anniversary edn. O'Reilly Media.

Liebetrau, T. and K. K. Christensen (2021). 'The Ontological Politics of Cyber Security: Emerging Agencies, Actors, Sites, and Spaces'. *European Journal of International Security* 6 (1): 25–43. https://doi.org/10.1017/eis.2020.10

Liebetrau, T. and L. Monsees (2022). 'Cybersecurity'. In *Elgar Encyclopedia of Technology and Politics*, edited by Andrea Ceron, 9–13. Edward Elgar Publishing.

Long, T., J. Johnson, A. Revelli, F. Plan and M. Barnhart (2024). 'APT45: North Korea's Digital Military Machine'. *Mandiant Google Cloud*, July 25. https://cloud.google.com/blog/topics/threat-intelligence/apt45-north-korea-digital-military-machine (accessed November 13, 2025).

Malwa, S. (2020). 'Hackers Drain $15 Million From "Unreleased" Yearn Finance Project'. *Decrypt*, September 29. https://decrypt.co/43203/hackers-drain-15-million-from-unreleased-yearn-finance-project (accessed November 13, 2025).

Marco De Vries (@paladin_marco) (2023). 'Today I messaged the SEAL911 hotline…' X, October 26. https://x.com/paladin_marco/status/1717482516578193661 (accessed November 13, 2025).

Marlinspike, M. (2022). 'My First Impressions of Web3'. *Moxie.org*, January 7. https://moxie.org/2022/01/07/web3-first-impressions.html (accessed November 13, 2025).

May, T. C. (1992a). 'The Crypto Anarchist Manifesto'. *Activism.net*, November 22. https://www.activism.net/cypherpunk/crypto-anarchy.html (accessed November 13, 2025).

May, T. C. (1992b). 'Libertaria in Cyberspace'. *Satoshi Nakamoto Institute*, September 1. https://nakamotoinstitute.org/libertaria-in-cyberspace (accessed November 13, 2025).

Maz, N. (2025). 'Bybit Hack 2025: How to Keep Your Crypto Safe from Cyber Threats'. *Atomic Wallet*, February 28. https://atomicwallet.io/academy/articles/bybit-hack-2025-how-to-keep-your-crypto-safe-from-cyber-threats (accessed November 13, 2025).

McKelvey, F. (2018). *Internet Daemons: Digital Communications Possessed*. University of Minnesota Press.

McPherson, A. (2025). 'On Hindsight and Risk'. *Privy*, February 27. https://www.privy.io/blog/bybit-lookback (accessed November 13, 2025).

Merkle, R. C. (1978). 'Secure Communications Over Insecure Channels'. *Communications of the ACM* 21 (4): 294–99. https://doi.org/10.1145/359460.359473

Michael Lewellen (@LewellenMichael) (2025). 'Today, I'm taking a stand…' X, January 16. https://x.com/LewellenMichael/status/1879921 399315193899 (accessed November 13, 2025).

Miller, M. S. (2017). 'Computer Security as the Future of Law'. Virtual lecture, August 11, 1997. Posted May 16, 2017. YouTube, 55:05. https://www.youtube.com/watch?v=kOFzisF7aNw (accessed November 13, 2025).

Miller, M. S. (n.d.). 'Posts – MARC'. https://marc.info/?a=109605695400003 &r=1&w=2 (accessed March 26, 2025).

Miller, M. and E. Drexler (1988). 'Markets and Computation: Agoric Open Systems'. In *The Ecology of Computation*, edited by B. Huberman, 133–76. Elsevier Science Publishers/North-Holland.

Monsees, L. (2020). 'Cryptoparties: Empowerment in Internet Security?' *Internet Policy Review* 9 (4). https://doi.org/10.14763/2020.4.1508

Monsees, L. (2021). *Crypto-Politics: Encryption and Democratic Practices in the Digital Era*. Routledge.

Mudit Gupta (@Mudit__Gupta) (2024). 'WazirX Hacked for Over \$230M USD…'. X, July 18. https://x.com/Mudit__Gupta/status/1813881385800913327 (accessed November 13, 2025).

Munro, I. and K. Kenny (2023). 'Whistleblower as Activist and Exile: The Case of Edward Snowden'. *Organization* 31(6): 994–1008. https://doi.org/10.1177/13505084231194824

Nabben, K. (2023a). 'Cryptoeconomics as Governance: An Intellectual History from "Crypto Anarchy" to "Cryptoeconomics"'. *Internet Histories* 7 (3): 254–76. https://doi.org/10.1080/24701475.2023.2183643

Nabben, K. (2023b). 'Governance by Algorithms, Governance of Algorithms: Human-Machine Politics in DAOs'. *PuntOorg International Journal* 8 (1): 36–54. https://doi.org/10.19245/25.05.pij.8.1.3

Nabben, K. (2023c). 'Web3 as "Self-Infrastructuring": The Challenge Is How'. *Big Data & Society* 10 (1). https://doi.org/10.1177/20539517231159002

Nabben, K. (2024). 'DAO Vulnerability Mapping: A Theoretical and Empirical Tool'. In *Decentralized Autonomous Organizations: Innovation and Vulnerability in the Digital Economy*, edited by S. V. Kerckhoven and U. W. Chohan. Routledge.

Nabben, K. and P. De Filippi (2023). 'SEAL DRILLS: Attack Simulations to Improve Web3 Security'. *Substack*. October 26. https://open.substack .com/pub/kelsienabben/p/the-chaos-team-attack-simulations?r=yper &utm_campaign=post&utm_medium=web (accessed November 1, 2025).

Nabben, K. and M. Zargham (2022). 'Permissionlessness'. *Internet Policy Review* 11 (2). https://doi.org/10.14763/2022.2.1656

Nakamoto, S. (2008) 'Bitcoin: A Peer-to-Peer Electronic Cash System'. *Bitbo.io*, https://bitcoinwhitepaper.co/ (accessed November 13, 2025).

Nakamoto, S. (n.d.). 'They Want to Delete the Wikipedia Article'. *BitcoinTalk* (forum). https://bitcointalk.org/index.php?topic=342.msg4508#msg4 508 (accessed September 9, 2022).

Nation Thailand (2024). 'Four Foreigners Arrested Over 8m Crypto Heist in Phuket', November 11. https://www.nationthailand.com/news/ general/40043178 (accessed November 13, 2025).

Nefture Security (2024). 'PlayDapp Exploit – Post-Mortem of a $290M Heist'. *Medium*, February 16. https://medium.com/nefture/playdapp -exploit-post-mortem-of-a-290m-heist-f6803349cde8 (accessed November 13, 2025).

Nelson, T. (1974). *Computer Lib/Dream Machines*. 1st edn. Self-published.

Nelson, T. H. (1999). 'The Unfinished Revolution and Xanadu'. *ACM Computing Surveys* (CSUR) 31 (4es): 37-es. https://doi.org/10.1145 /345966.346039

Nicolas Bacca (@BTChip) (2025a). 'On-chain heroes...' X, January 23. https://x.com/BTChip/status/1882508742790697243 (accessed November 13, 2025).

Nicolas Bacca (@BTChip) (2025b). 'Thanks to @BrutalTrade...' X, January 25. https://x.com/BTChip/status/1883288953987666314 (accessed November 13, 2025).

Nissenbaum, H. (2004). 'Hackers and the Contested Ontology of Cyberspace'. *New Media & Society* 6 (2): 195–217. https://doi.org/10 .1177/1461444804041445

Nissenbaum, H. (2009). *Privacy in Context*. Stanford Law Books.

NIST (National Institute of Standards and Technology – US Department of Commerce) (n.d.). 'Cyber Attack'. *Computer Security Resource Centre*. https://csrc.nist.gov/glossary/term/cyber_attack (accessed November 13, 2025)

O'Dwyer, R. (2015). 'The Revolution Will (Not) Be Decentralised: Blockchains'. *Platform Cooperativism Consortium*, June 11. https:// resources.platform.coop/resources/the-revolution-will-not-be -decentralised-blockchains

Omniscia (2023). 'Euler Finance Incident Post-Mortem'. *Medium*, March 13. https://medium.com/@omniscia.io/euler-finance-incident-post -mortem-1ce077c28454 (accessed November 13, 2025).

OpenZeppelin (2017). 'The Parity Wallet Hack Explained'. *OpenZeppelin*, July 19. https://blog.openzeppelin.com/on-the-parity-wallet-multisig -hack-405a8c12e8f7 (accessed November 13, 2025).

Park, J. (2021). 'The Lazarus Group: The Cybercrime Syndicate Financing the North Korea State'. *Harvard International Review* 42 (2): 34–39.

pcaversaccio [sudo rm -rf --no-preserve-root /] (@pcaversaccio) (2023). 'Today is a historic moment for SEAL 911…' X, September 26. https://x.com/pcaversaccio/status/1706713159887716700 (accessed November 13, 2025).

pcaversaccio [sudo rm -rf --no-preserve-root /] (@pcaversaccio) (2024a). 'If You Build a Crypto Project for the Masses…' X, July 14. https://x.com/pcaversaccio/status/1812446005394087991

pcaversaccio [sudo rm -rf --no-preserve-root /] (@pcaversaccio) (2024b). 'Over the past few years…' X, October 16. https://x.com/pcaversaccio/status/1846602838127849726 (accessed November 13, 2025).

pcaversaccio [sudo rm -rf --no-preserve-root /] (@pcaversaccio) (2024c). '3/ WHAT can SEAL 911 help with…' X, August 7. https://x.com/pcaversaccio/status/1821090465426395281

pcaversaccio [sudo rm -rf --no-preserve-root /] (@pcaversaccio) (2024d). '1/ Exactly 1 year ago…' X, August 7. https://x.com/pcaversaccio/status/1821090459239792683 (accessed November 13, 2025).

pcaversaccio [sudo rm -rf --no-preserve-root /] (@pcaversaccio) (2024e). 'I firmly believe that using Tornado Cash…' X, August 29. https://x.com/pcaversaccio/status/1829158484727796021 (accessed November 13, 2025).

pcaversaccio [sudo rm -rf --no-preserve-root /] (@pcaversaccio) (2024f). 'This has been a white hat rescue…' X, March 21. https://x.com/pcaversaccio/status/1770840376636481833 (accessed November 13, 2025).

pcaversaccio [sudo rm -rf --no-preserve-root /] (@pcaversaccio) (2024g). 'If someone asks how it looks like to be a SEAL 911 member…' X, September 5. https://x.com/pcaversaccio/status/1831645124066951343 (accessed November 13, 2025).

pcaversaccio [sudo rm -rf --no-preserve-root /] (@pcaversaccio) (2024h). 'We're fucking drowning in seal 911 tickets…' X, October 6. https://x.com/pcaversaccio/status/1842860274014917115 (accessed November 13, 2025).

pcaversaccio [sudo rm -rf --no-preserve-root /] (@pcaversaccio) (2024i). '4/ WHO is behind SEAL 911…' X, August 7. https://x.com/pcaversaccio/status/1821090467489972527 (accessed November 13, 2025).

pcaversaccio (2024). 'The Ethereum Cypherpunk Manifesto'. *HackMD*, last edited April 17. https://hackmd.io/@pcaversaccio/the-ethereum-cypherpunk-manifesto (accessed November 13, 2025).

pcaversaccio [sudo rm -rf --no-preserve-root /] (@pcaversaccio) (2025). 'It's been an absolutely wild week…' X, January 25. https://x.com/

pcaversaccio/status/1883106722274779301 (accessed November 13, 2025).

pcaversaccio [sudo rm -rf --no-preserve-root /] (@pcaversaccio) (2025b). 'Bybit effectively signed an untrusted delegatecall...' X, March 5. https://x.com/pcaversaccio/status/1897358972614590764 (accessed November 13, 2025).

pcaversaccio [sudo rm -rf --no-preserve-root /] (@pcaversaccio) (2025a). 'It has taken 19 days...' X, March 6. https://x.com/pcaversaccio/status/1897666468327588089 (accessed November 13, 2025).

pcaversaccio (n.d.). '1inch-analysis.app – A DPRK Trojan Horse'. *HackMD*, last edited March 28, 2025. https://hackmd.io/@pcaversaccio/1inch-analysis-app-a-dprk-trojan-horse (accessed April 11, 2025).

Pearl, M. (2025). 'Putting Lipstick on a Pig: A Deep Dive into Pig Butchering Scams in Crypto'. *Cyvers*, https://substack.com/redirect/25239d5c-20d2-40ab-ad9c-e6a1a4d49580?j=eyJ1IjoieXBlciJ9.L_301DOYhrs9s5-LKs NTgTX1oGy21qvYWhfwcaa6UNM (accessed November 13, 2025).

Perdana, A., M. E. Aminanto and B. Anggorojati (2024). 'Hack, Heist, and Havoc: The Lazarus Group's Triple Threat to Global Cybersecurity'. *Journal of Information Technology Teaching Cases*. https://doi.org/10.1177/20438869241303941

Perens, B. (1999). 'The Open Source Definition'. In *Open Sources: Voices from the Open Source Revolution, vol. 1*, edited by C. DiBona and S. Ockman, 171–88. O'Reilly Media.

Pierce, W. H. (1965). *Failure-Tolerant Computer Design*. Academic Press.

Pink, S., H. Horst, J. Postill, L. Hjorth, T. Lewis and J. Tacchi (2016). *Digital Ethnography: Principles and Practice*. SAGE Publications Ltd.

Protos (@Protos) (2025). 'ALERT: Critical Vulnerability (CVE-2025-27840) Found...' X, April 15. https://x.com/Protos/status/1912148405943480814 (accessed November 13, 2025).

Radiant Capital (@RDNTCapital@RDNTCapital@RDNTCapital) (2024a). 'On October 16, 2024, Radiant Capital experienced...' X, October 18 https://x.com/RDNTCapital/status/1847121278974480779 (accessed November 13, 2025).

Radiant Capital (2024b). 'Radiant Capital Post-Mortem'. *Medium*, October 18. https://medium.com/@RadiantCapital/radiant-post-mortem-fecd6cd38081 (accessed November 13, 2025).

RAND Corporation (n.d.) 'Paul Baran'. *RAND Corporation*. https://www.rand.org/pubs/authors/b/baran_paul.html (accessed July 6, 2023).

Rankin, J. L. (2018). *A People's History of Computing in the United States*. Harvard University Press.

Raymond, E. S. and G. L. Steele (eds) (1991). *The New Hacker's Dictionary*. MIT Press.

Raymond, G. (2025). 'We Have Invented a Unique Organisational Model for Intervening in Cryptocurrency Ransom'. *The Big Whale*, January 24. https://en.thebigwhale.io/article-en/nicolas-bacca-we-have-invented-a-unique-organisational-model-for-intervening-in-cryptocurrency-ransomware (accessed November 13, 2025).

Reguerra, E. (2025). 'Ethical Hacker Intercepts $2.6M in Morpho Labs Exploit'. *Cointelegraph*, April 11. https://cointelegraph.com/news/white-hat-intercepts-2-million-morpho-blue-hack (accessed November 13, 2025).

Rekt News (@RektHQ) (2021). 'Punk IS dead…' X, August 13. https://x.com/RektHQ/status/1426141203796475905 (accessed November 13, 2025).

Rekt News (2021). 'Punk Protocol'. https://www.rekt.news (accessed March 31, 2025).

Rekt News (n.d.a). 'Rekt'. https://www.rekt.news/ (accessed March 26, 2025).

Rekt News (n.d.b). 'Leaderboard'. https://rekt.news/leaderboard (accessed March 26, 2025).

Rennie, E. (2024). 'Climate Change and the Legitimacy of Bitcoin: Legitimacy and Delegitimisation in Relation to Distributed Ledgers'. *Cryptoeconomic Systems* 3 (1). https://doi.org/10.21428/58320208.d891046f

Rettig, R., M. Mosier and K. Gilman (2024). 'Genuine DeFi as Critical Infrastructure: A Conceptual Framework for Combating Illicit Finance Activity in Decentralized Finance'. *SSRN*. https://doi.org/10.2139/ssrn.4607332

Rivest, R. L., A. Shamir and L. Adleman (1978). 'A Method for Obtaining Digital Signatures and Public-Key Cryptosystems'. *Communications of the ACM* 21 (2): 120–26. https://doi.org/10.1145/359340.359342 (accessed November 13, 2025).

Ronin (@Ronin_Network) (2022). 'There has been a security breach…' X, March 29. https://x.com/Ronin_Network/status/1508828719711879168 (accessed November 13, 2025).

Ropek, L. (2025). 'The FBI Hijacked and Ran a Dark Web Money Laundering Operation Called "ElonmuskWHM"'. *Gizmodo*, April 8. https://gizmodo.com/the-fbi-hijacked-and-ran-a-dark-web-money-laundering-operation-called-elonmuskwhm-2000586515 (accessed November 13, 2025).

Sadowski, J. and K. Beegle (2023). 'Expansive and Extractive Networks of Web3'. *Big Data & Society* 10 (1). https://doi.org/10.1177/20539517231159629

Safe Global (n.d.). 'feat: Show message and domain hash by schmanu · Pull Request #4394 · safe-global/safe-wallet-monorepo'. *GitHub*. https://

github.com/safe-global/safe-wallet-monorepo/pull/4394   (accessed November 13, 2025).

Safe (2025). 'February 28th, 2025: Statement by the Safe Ecosystem Foundation'. February 28. https://safe.global/blog/safe-ecosystem -foundation-statement (accessed November 13, 2025).

Safe.eth (@safe) (2024). 'Statement from Safe…' X, October 18. https://x. com/safe/status/1847253904246878553 (accessed November 13, 2025).

Sandor, K. (2025). 'Ledger Co-Founder's Kidnapping Highlights Threat of Crypto Robberies'. *CoinDesk*, January 24. https://www.coindesk .com/policy/2025/01/24/ledger-co-founder-s-kidnapping-sheds-light-on -soaring-crypto-robberies (accessed November 13, 2025).

Scam Sniffer, Web3 Anti-Scam (@realScamSniffer) (2024). '43 mins ago, someone lost 12,083 spWETH ($32.43M)…'. X, September 28. https://x.com/realScamSniffer/status/1839923975184625832 (accessed November 13, 2025).

Scam Sniffer (2025). 'Scam Sniffer 2024: Web3 Phishing Attacks'. *Scam Sniffer*, January 3. https://drops.scamsniffer.io/scam-sniffer-2024 -web3-phishing-attacks-wallet-drainers-drain-494-million   (accessed November 13, 2025).

Security Alliance (@_SEAL_Org) (2025a). 'The SEAL Whitehat Safe Harbor Agreement just turned 1…' X, February 19. https://x.com/_ SEAL_Org/status/1892250406719271222 (accessed November 13, 2025).

Security Alliance (@_SEAL_Org) (2025b). 'NEWS: @pendle_fi just adopted the SEAL Whitehat Safe Harbor Agreement…' X, March 17. https://x.com/_SEAL_Org/status/1901654210782920902   (accessed November 13, 2025).

Security Alliance (2024). 'DPRK #OpenToWork'. *GitHub*, October 24. https://www.securityalliance.org/news/DPRK_OpenToWork   (accessed November 13, 2025).

Security Alliance (n.d.a). Security Alliance. https://www.securityalliance .org/ (accessed 1 April 2025).

Security Alliance (n.d.b). Security Alliance, Intel. https://www .securityalliance.org/intel (accessed November 13, 2025).

Security Alliance (n.d.c). 'Security Alliance (SEAL) Whitehat Safe Harbor Agreement & Related Materials'. *GitHub*. https://github.com/security -alliance/safe-harbor/blob/main/documents/agreement.pdf   (accessed April 29, 2025).

Security Alliance/SEAL 911 (n.d.). 'Seal-911 Code of Conduct'. *GitHub*, last updated March 4, 2024. https://github.com/security-alliance/seal

-911/blob/main/CODE_OF_CONDUCT.md (accessed November 13, 2025).

Shin, L. (2025a). 'How the $1.5 Billion Bybit Hack Could Have Been Prevented'. *Unchained*, February 28. https://unchainedcrypto.com/how-the-1-5-billion-bybit-hack-could-have-been-prevented (accessed 13 November, 2025).

Shin, L. (2025b). 'North Korean Hackers Are Winning. Is the Crypto Industry Ready to Stop Them?' *Unchained*, February 25. https://unchainedcrypto.com/north-korean-hackers-are-winning-is-the-crypto-industry-ready-to-stop-them (accessed November 13, 2025).

Shires, J. (2018). 'Enacting Expertise: Ritual and Risk in Cybersecurity'. *Politics and Governance* 6 (2): 31–40. https://doi.org/10.17645/pag.v6i2.1329

Siers, R. (2017). 'North Korea: The Cyber Wild Card 2.0'. *Journal of Law & Cyber Warfare* 6(1): 155–65.

Simondon, G. (2017). *On the Mode of Existence of Technical Objects*. Minneapolis, MN: Univocal Publishing.

Socket Tech (2024). 'Reimbursements for Affected Users'. https://sockettech.notion.site/Reimbursements-for-Affected-Users-b4bda067991048669c03604f91e4e262 (accessed April 7, 2025).

Solidus Labs (n.d.). 'US Regulators Broke Crypto Enforcement Records in 2022'. https://www.soliduslabs.com/research/2023-crypto-enforcement-trends (accessed November 13, 2025).

Star, S. L. (1999). 'The Ethnography of Infrastructure'. *American Behavioral Scientist* 43 (3): 377–91. https://doi.org/10.1177/00027649921955326

Star, S. L. and J. R. Griesemer (1989). 'Institutional Ecology, "Translations" and Boundary Objects: Amateurs and Professionals in Berkeley's Museum of Vertebrate Zoology, 1907–39'. *Social Studies of Science*, 19 (3), 387–420. (original work published 1989).

Star, S. L. and G. C. Bowker (2010) 'How to Infrastructure'. In *Handbook of New Media: Social Shaping and Social Consequences of ICTs, Updated Student Edition*, edited by L. A. Lievrouw and S. Livingstone, 230–45. SAGE Publications.

Star, S. L. and K. Ruhleder (1996). 'Steps Toward an Ecology of Infrastructure: Design and Access for Large Information Spaces'. *Information Systems Research* 7 (1): 111–34. https://doi.org/10.1287/isre.7.1.111

Stringham, E. P. (2017). 'Private Governance'. In *The Routledge Handbook of Libertarianism*, edited by J. Brennan, B. van der Vossen, anad D. Schmidtz. https://doi.org/10.4324/9781317486794

Stevens, C. (2020). 'Assembling Cybersecurity: The Politics and Materiality of Technical Malware Reports and the Case of Stuxnet'. *Contemporary

Security Policy 41 (1): 129–52. https://doi.org/10.1080/13523260.2019.1675258

Swartz, L. (2017). 'Blockchain Dreams: Imagining Techno-Economic Alternatives after Bitcoin'. In *Another Economy is Possible: Culture and Economy in a Time of Crisis*, edited by M. Castellas, 82–105. Polity Press.

Swartz, L. (2018). 'What Was Bitcoin, What Will It Be? The Techno-Economic Imaginaries of a New Money Technology'. *Cultural Studies* 32 (4): 623–50. https://doi.org/10.1080/09502386.2017.1416420

Tanczer, L. M. (2020). '50 Shades of Hacking: How IT and Cybersecurity Industry Actors Perceive Good, Bad, and Former Hackers'. *Contemporary Security Policy* 41 (1): 108–28. https://doi.org/10.1080/13523260.2019.1669336

tanuki42 (@tanuki42_) (2025). 'Meet Nick Franklin @0xNickLFranklin – Blockchain Security Engineer...' X, March 26. https://x.com/tanuki42_/status/1905003045433290940 (accessed November 13, 2025).

Tarnoff, B. (2022). *Internet for the People*. Verso.

Tay (@tayvano_) (2023). 'The blockchain is a public ledger...' X, September 13. https://x.com/tayvano_/status/1701958608001638781 (accessed November 13, 2025).

Tay (@tayvano_) (2024a). 'Background on the referenced hacks...' X, October 20. https://x.com/tayvano_/status/1847877011462901915 (accessed November 13, 2025).

Tay (@tayvano_) (2024b). 'Dear people who see stories abt people who had their keys drained today...' X, May 8. https://x.com/tayvano_/status/1788037679655063560 (accessed November 13, 2025).

Tay (@tayvano_) (2024c). 'Crypto folks already know...' X, July 8. https://x.com/tayvano_/status/1810455262320570416 (accessed November 13, 2025).

Tay (@tayvano_) (2025a). 'it would be super cool if this actually mattered...' X, April 15. https://x.com/tayvano_/status/1912259737812627519 (accessed November 13, 2025).

Tay (@tayvano_) (2025b). 'People keep calling this the "largest crypto hack ever"...' X, February 22. https://x.com/tayvano_/status/1893139888226046145 (accessed November 13, 2025).

Tay (@tayvano_) (2025c). 'And obvs this dwarfs the prior biggest crypto hacks...' X, February 22. https://x.com/tayvano_/status/1893139894656213513 (accessed November 13, 2025).

Tay (@tayvano_) (2025d). '150,000+ ETH 7k+ addresses 10k+ transactions...' X, February 27. https://x.com/tayvano_/status/1894906640375382024 (accessed November 13, 2025).

Tay (@tayvano_) (2025e). 'In 10 days flat, DPRK has bridged all ~500,000 ETH...' X, March 4. https://x.com/tayvano_/status/1896761187603497289 (accessed November 13, 2025).

Tayvano (2025a). 'Tayvano/lazarus-bluenoroff-research' [computer software]. (Original work published 2022 on GitHub). https://github.com/tayvano/lazarus-bluenoroff-research (accessed November 13, 2025).

Tayvano (2025b). 'Bybit Incident Investigation Preliminary Report', posted by Tayvano/lazarus-bluenoroff-research on GitHub. https://github.com/tayvano/lazarus-bluenoroff-research/blob/main/pdfs/2025-02-24_Bybit-Incident-Investigation_Preliminary-Report_Verichains.pdf (accessed November 13, 2025).

The Red Guild (n.d.). 'Phishing Dojo by The Red Guild'. https://phishing.therektgames.com (accessed 2 April, 2025).

There.Is.Now.Alternative (@tzhen) (2024). 'Chapter 2 Co-building the TEE Stack...' X, November 10. https://x.com/tzhen/status/1855563459821478357/photo/1 (accessed November 13, 2025).

Troncoso, C., M. Isaakidis, G. Denezis and H. Halpin (2017). 'Systematizing Decentralization and Privacy: Lessons from 15 Years of Research and Deployments'. *Proceedings on Privacy Enhancing Technologies* 2017 (4): 329–44. https://doi.org/10.48550/arXiv.1704.08065

Turner, F. (2008). *From Counterculture to Cyberculture*. University of Chicago Press. https://press.uchicago.edu/ucp/books/book/chicago/F/bo3773600.html

US Attorney's Office (Southern District of New York) (2023). 'Former Security Engineer for International Technology Company Pleads Guilty to Hacking Two Decentralized Cryptocurrency Exchanges'. *US Department of Justice*, December 14. https://www.justice.gov/usao-sdny/pr/former-security-engineer-international-technology-company-pleads-guilty-hacking-two (accessed November 13, 2025).

US Attorney's Office (District of Massachusetts) (2024). 'Eighteen Individuals and Entities Charged in International Operation Targeting Widespread Fraud and Manipulation in the Cryptocurrency Markets'. https://www.justice.gov/usao-ma/pr/eighteen-individuals-and-entities-charged-international-operation-targeting-widespread (accessed November 1, 2025).

US Attorney's Office (Southern District of New York) (2024). 'Former Security Engineer Sentenced to Three Years in Prison for Hacking Two Decentralized Cryptocurrency Exchanges'. *US Department of Justice*, April 12. https://www.justice.gov/usao-sdny/pr/former-security-engineer-sentenced-three-years-prison-hacking-two-decentralized (accessed November 13, 2025).

US Attorney's Office (2025). 'Additional 12 Defendants Charged in RICO Conspiracy for over $263 Million Cryptocurrency Thefts, Money Laundering, Home Break-Ins'. *United States Department of Justice*, May 15. https://www.justice.gov/usao-dc/pr/additional-12-defendants-charged-rico-conspiracy-over-263-million-cryptocurrency-thefts (accessed 13 November, 2025).

US Attorney's Office (Eastern District of Kentucky) (2025). 'International Crypto Vendor Sentenced for Money Laundering Conspiracy'. *United States Department of Justice*, January 17. https://www.justice.gov/usao-edky/pr/international-crypto-vendor-sentenced-money-laundering-conspiracy (accessed 13 November, 2025).

US Department of Justice (2018). 'North Korean Regime-Backed Programmer Charged With Conspiracy to Conduct Multiple Cyber Attacks and Intrusions'. *Office of Public Affairs*, September 6. https://www.justice.gov/archives/opa/pr/north-korean-regime-backed-programmer-charged-conspiracy-conduct-multiple-cyber-attacks-and (accessed 13 November, 2025).

US Department of Justice (2023). 'Justice Department Announces Court-Authorized Action'. *Office of Public Affairs*, October 18. https://www.justice.gov/archives/opa/pr/justice-department-announces-court-authorized-action-disrupt-illicit-revenue-generation (accessed 13 November, 2025).

US Department of Justice (2024). 'Twelve Defendants Sentenced for Violent Home Invasion Robberies to Steal Cryptocurrency'. *Office of Public Affairs*, September 13. https://www.justice.gov/archives/opa/pr/twelve-defendants-sentenced-violent-home-invasion-robberies-steal-cryptocurrency (accessed 13 November, 2025).

US Department of Justice (2025). 'Nationwide Actions to Combat North Korean Remote Information Technology Workers' Illicit Revenue Generation Schemes'. *Office of Public Affairs*, June 30. https://www.justice.gov/opa/pr/justice-department-announces-coordinated-nationwide-actions-combat-north-korean-remote (accessed 13 November, 2025).

US Department of State (2025). 'Joint Statement on Cryptocurrency Thefts by the Democratic People's Republic of Korea'. January 14. https://2021-2025.state.gov/office-of-the-spokesperson/releases/2025/01/joint-statement-on-cryptocurrency-thefts-by-the-democratic-peoples-republic-of-korea-and-public-private-collaboration/ (accessed 13 November, 2025).

US Department of the Treasury (2019). 'Treasury Sanctions North Korean State-Sponsored Malicious Cyber Groups'. September 13. https://home.treasury.gov/news/press-releases/sm774 (accessed 13 November, 2025).

US Department of the Treasury (2022). 'U.S. Treasury Sanctions Notorious Virtual Currency Mixer Tornado Cash'. August 8. https://home.treasury.gov/news/press-releases/jy0916 (accessed 13 November, 2025).

US Department of the Treasury (2025). 'Tornado Cash Delisting'. February 8. https://home.treasury.gov/news/press-releases/sb0057 (accessed 13 November, 2025).

US Securities and Exchange Commission (2024). 'SEC Charges Three So-Called Market Makers and Nine Individuals in Crackdown on Manipulation of Crypto Assets Offered and Sold as Securities'. October 9. https://www.sec.gov/newsroom/press-releases/2024-166 (accessed 13 November, 2025).

Unchained (2025). 'The Chopping Block: Crypto's Worst Week? Bybit Hack, Libra Scandal, & The Memecoin Reckoning'. February 23. https://unchainedcrypto.com/the-chopping-block-cryptos-worst-week-bybit-hack-libra-scandal-the-memecoin-reckoning (accessed 13 November, 2025).

United Nations Security Council (2023). 'Final Report of the Panel of Experts Submitted Pursuant to Resolution 2627 (2022)'. March 7. https://main.un.org/securitycouncil/en/sanctions/1718/panel_experts/reports (accessed November 13, 2025).

United States District Court of California (2019). 'Michael Terpin v. AT and T Inc et al, No. 2:2018cv06975 – Document 29 (C.D. Cal. 2019)'. https://law.justia.com/cases/federal/district-courts/california/cacdce/2:2018cv06975/719795/29/ (accessed November 13, 2025).

Urbanik, M.-M. and R. A. Roks (2020). 'GangstaLife: Fusing Urban Ethnography with Netnography'. *Qualitative Sociology* 43 (2): 213–33. https://doi.org/10.1007/s11133-020-09445-0

Vinsel, L. and A. L. Russell (2020). *The Innovation Delusion: How Our Obsession with the New Has Disrupted the Work That Matters Most.* Crown Currency.

Vitalik.eth (@VitalikButerin) (2022). 'Thread: Some Still Open Contradictions…' X, May 16. https://twitter.com/VitalikButerin/status/1526378787855736832 (accessed November 13, 2025).

Voshmgir, S. and M. Zargham (2020). 'Foundations of Cryptoeconomic Systems'. WU Vienna University of Economics and Business Working Paper Series, Institute for Cryptoeconomics, Interdisciplinary Research 1.

Voskuil, E., J. Chiang and A. Taaki (2020). *Cryptoeconomics: Fundamental Principles of Bitcoin.* Bowker Identifier Services.

Warwick, K. (2019). 'Synthetix Response to Oracle Incident'. *Synthetix,* June 25. https://blog.synthetix.io/response-to-oracle-incident (accessed November 13, 2025).

Weiss, B. and J. J. Roberts (2025). 'Inside the $400 Million Coinbase Breach: An Indian Call Center and Teenage Hackers'. *Fortune Crypto*, May 29. https://fortune.com/crypto/2025/05/29/coinbase-hack-the -community-taskus-bpos-teenagers/ (accessed August 6, 2025).

Wendl, M., M. H. Doan and R. Sassen (2023). 'The Environmental Impact of Cryptocurrencies Using Proof of Work and Proof of Stake Consensus Algorithms: A Systematic Review'. *Journal of Environmental Management* 326: 116530. https://doi.org/10.1016/j.jenvman.2022 .116530

Whatmore, R. (2016). *What is Intellectual History?* John Wiley & Sons.

White, G. (2022). *The Lazarus Heist: Based on the No 1 Hit Podcast.* Penguin UK.

Whittaker, Z. (2024). 'Authorities Catch "SMS Blaster" Gang...' *TechCrunch*, November 25. https://techcrunch.com/2024/11/25/ authorities-catch-sms-blaster-gang-that-drove-around-bangkok-sending -thousands-of-phishing-messages (accessed November 13, 2025).

Williamson, M. J. (1974). 'Non-Secret Encryption Using a Finite Field'. GCHQ internal note, 21 January. https://cryptocellar.org/cesg/secenc .pdf (accessed November 13, 2025).

Wolff, J. (2016). 'What We Talk About When We Talk About Cybersecurity'. *Internet Policy Review* 5 (3): 1–13. https://doi.org/10.14763/2016.3.43

Wood, A. (2025). 'Who Is Andean Medjedovic, the Alleged $48M KyberSwap Hacker?' *Cointelegraph*, February 4. https://cointelegraph .com/news/andean-medjedovic-kyberswap-alleged-hacker (accessed November 13, 2025).

Yearn (n.d.). 'Yearn-Security/Disclosures at Master · yearn/yearn-security'. *GitHub*. Last updated November 14, 2024. https://github.com/yearn/ yearn-security/tree/master/disclosures (accessed November 13, 2025).

Yogi (@HouseofYogiX) (2025). 'THORChain just helped North Korea launder $605 million...' X, March 4. https://x.com/HouseofYogiX/ status/1896787435662553216 (accessed November 13, 2025).

Yoo, C. S. (2018). 'Paul Baran, Network Theory, and the Past, Present, and Future of the Internet'. *Colorado Technology Law Journal* 17 (1): 161–86. https://doi.org/10.2139/ssrn.3317642

Yost, J. R. (2015a). 'Martin Hellman – A.M. Turing Award Laureate'. *Association for Computing Machinery*. https://amturing.acm.org/award _winners/hellman_4055781.cfm (accessed November 13, 2025).

Yost, J. R. (2015b). 'Whitfield Diffie – A.M. Turing Award Laureate'. *Association for Computing Machinery*. https://amturing.acm.org/award _winners/diffie_8371646.cfm (accessed November 13, 2025).

Yun, Y. (2025). 'THORChain at crossroads: Decentralization clashes with illicit activity'. *Cointelegraph*, March 11. https://cointelegraph

.com/news/thorchain-crossroads-decentralized-collides-illicit-activity (accessed November 13, 2025).

ZachXBT (@zachxbt) (2022). 'A smart decision here by the hacker...' X, July 6. https://x.com/zachxbt/status/1544797170762760192 (accessed November 13, 2025).

ZachXBT (@zachxbt) (2024). 'How Lazarus Group Laundered $200M from 25+ Crypto Hacks to Fiat from 2020–2023'. *Investigations by ZachXBT (Mirror.xyz)*, April 29. https://zachxbt.mirror.xyz/B0-UJt xN41cJhpPtKv0v2LZ8u-0PwZ4ecMPEdX4l8vE (accessed November 13, 2025).

ZachXBT (@zachxbt) (2025a). '@MickiCrossChain One of my biggest regrets...' X, January 20. https://x.com/zachxbt/status/1881268125414691275 (accessed November 13, 2025).

ZachXBT (@zachxbt) (2025b). 'Lazarus Group just connected the Bybit hack...' X, February 22. https://x.com/zachxbt/status/1893211577836302365 (accessed November 13, 2025).

ZachXBT (@zachxbt) (2025c). 'Today when laundering funds for the Bybit Hack...' X, February 24. https://x.com/zachxbt/status/1894004267553304723 (accessed November 13, 2025).

ZachXBT (@zachxbt) (2025d). '1/ An unnamed source recently compromised a DPRK IT worker device...' X, August 13. https://x.com/zachxbt/status/1955613912201896113 (accessed November 13, 2025).

ZachXBT (@zachxbt) (2025e). '1/ My recent investigation uncovered more than $16.58M in payments...' X, July 2. https://x.com/zachxbt/status/1940388827392344261 (accessed November 13, 2025).

Zuboff, S. (2015). 'Big Other: Surveillance Capitalism and the Prospects of an Information Civilization'. *Journal of Information Technology* 30 (1): 75–89. https://doi.org/10.1057/jit.2015.5

Index

EU authorised representative for GPSR:
Easy Access System Europe, Mustamäe tee 50,
10621 Tallinn, Estonia
gpsr.requests@easproject.com

www.ingramcontent.com/pod-product-compliance
Ingram Content Group UK Ltd.
Pitfield, Milton Keynes, MK11 3LW, UK
UKHW021812150726
7214IPUK00004B/13